Achieving ISO/IEC 20000
Integrated service management

The 'Achieving ISO/IEC 20000' series

This publication is the ninth in a series of ten publications related to ISO/IEC 20000. Each publication provides advice on different aspects of ISO/IEC 20000. The books in the 'Achieving ISO/IEC 20000' series are:

Management decisions and documentation (BIP 0030)

Why people matter (BIP 0031)

Making metrics work (BIP 0032)

Managing end-to-end service (BIP 0033)

Finance for service managers (BIP 0034)

Enabling change (BIP 0035)

Keeping the service going (BIP 0036)

Capacity management (BIP 0037)

Integrated service management (BIP 0038)

The differences between BS 15000 and ISO/IEC 20000 (BIP 0039)

This series provides practical guidance and advice on introducing IT service management best practice in accordance with ISO/IEC 20000. More details on the content of each publication are given in *Books in the 'Achieving ISO/IEC 20000' series*, at the end of this book.

Although security issues are covered in ISO/IEC 20000, the 'Achieving ISO/IEC 20000' series does not cover security requirements. Information on security can be found in the BSI publications that are listed in the *Bibliography* in Appendix B.

Other publications

BSI also publishes:

A managers' guide to service management (BIP 0005) is intended for managers who are new to support services or who are faced with major changes to their existing support facility. This book takes the form of informative explanations, guidance and recommendations.

IT service management – Self-assessment workbook (BIP 0015) is an easy to use checklist that complements ISO/IEC 20000 and is designed to assist an organization's internal assessment of their services and the extent to which they conform to the specified requirements in ISO/IEC 20000.

Achieving ISO/IEC 20000
Integrated service management

Dr Jenny Dugmore and Shirley Lacy

Business
Information

First published in the UK in 2006
Reprinted in 2007

by
BSI
389 Chiswick High Road
London W4 4AL

Typeset in Frutiger by Typobatics Limited
Printed in Great Britain by MPG Books Limited

British Library Cataloguing in Publication Data
A catalogue record for this book is available from the British Library

ISBN 978-0-580-44642-9

Contents

Foreword

The Introduction of ISO/IEC 20000-1 states that *'This standard promotes the adoption of an integrated process approach to effectively deliver managed services to meet the business and customer requirements'.*

This book reflects the importance placed by ISO/IEC 20000 on understanding and managing the interfaces between processes so that they are fully integrated. It reflects the top-down management system approach of the ISO/IEC 20000 requirements.

It also covers the management system requirements of ISO/IEC 20000, in particular management commitment and the Plan-Do-Check-Act cycle and the management process responsibilities around implementing a new or changed system and the role this plays in integrating service management.

Organizations reap the full benefits of service management only by ensuring that information flows from one process to another. Only by recognizing that there is a need to permanently seek and implement better ways of working will services continue to meet the customer's business needs. In contrast, when service management processes are implemented, followed or changed in isolation, they provide much less value and are frequently a bureaucratic overhead that does not deliver value for money. The lack of management commitment means that processes may actually conflict, or never really become established at all.

Dr Jenny Dugmore

Acknowledgements

This book has been produced with the input and assistance of people involved in the practical aspects of delivering services across all sectors. We would like to thank them for sharing their views and providing constructive criticism, case studies and practical techniques.

It is not possible to list all those who have helped, but particular thanks goes to:

Barbara Eastman; Peter Lickiss; Alan Miller of BSI Consumer Policy Committee; Alison Holt of Synergy International Limited; Bridget Veitch of Xansa, Maggie Kneller; David Bickett of Deloittes Enterprise Risk Management; David Clifford of pro-attivo; Don Page of Marval; Finbarr Callum of The Grey Matters; Gerald Mulhern of Aperitil Consultancy Limited; Hella Schrader of the Financial Times; Hilary Faul of Siemens Business Services; Ivor Macfarlane of Guillemot Rock; John Groom of West Groom Consulting; Louise Howson of Xansa; Lynda Cooper of Fox IT; Majid Iqbal of Carnegie Mellon University; Ro Gorell of Ascent2Change; Steve Harcus of Siemens Business Services; and Tony Jenkins of DOMAINetc.

Finally, we would like to thank Simone Levy and Kieran Parkinson of BSI for their support, helpful suggestions, tact and patience with the production of the 'Achieving ISO/IEC 20000' series.

INTRODUCTION

What is ISO/IEC 20000?

ISO/IEC 20000 is the first IT service management process standard to be produced by the International Organization for Standardization (ISO), and is based on the knowledge and experience gained by experts working in the field.

ISO/IEC 20000 was produced by Technical Committee ISO/IEC JTC 1 /SC 7, *Software and system engineering*, and was based on BS 15000, which was produced by BSI Technical Committee BDD/3, *Information services management*.

ISO/IEC 20000 is in two parts.

*   ISO/IEC 20000-1 is a specification containing requirements that must be met in order to achieve ISO/IEC 20000.

*   ISO/IEC 20000-2 is a code of practice on how to achieve the requirements in ISO/IEC 20000-1.

The compulsory requirements in Part 1 (i.e. ISO/IEC 20000-1) are applicable to service providers of all sizes and types, regardless of whether the organization is public or private sector, internal or external. The recommendations in Part 2 (i.e. ISO/IEC 20000-2) are optional approaches to achieving the requirements in Part 1. Although optional, the recommendations are also practical and proven methods that are normally appropriate.

The purpose of ISO/IEC 20000

ISO/IEC 20000 provides the basis for assessing whether service providers have best practice, reliable, repeatable and measurable processes applied consistently across their organization. As a process-based standard the requirements are independent of organizational structure or of the tools used to automate the service management processes. ISO/IEC 20000-1 provides the basis for formal certification schemes and other audits.

The 'Achieving ISO/IEC 20000' series

The 'Achieving ISO/IEC 20000' series is designed to explain the requirements of ISO/IEC 20000. An abstract of the ISO/IEC 20000 clauses that are most relevant to the topic of 'Integrated service management' is given in Appendix A. Also, Table 1 provides a clause-by-clause guide to the content of each of the books in the 'Achieving ISO/IEC 20000' series.

This ninth publication in the 'Achieving ISO/IEC 20000' series includes example metrics and audit evidence, with practical hints, tips and techniques that will help a service provider achieve the requirements in clauses 3, 4 and 5.

As with the other publications in this series, the recommendations given in ISO/IEC 20000-2 are also described. Many of the case studies and examples in this publication have been based on experiences with BS 15000, which was the precursor to ISO/IEC 20000.

Additional advice

Service providers aiming to achieve ISO/IEC 20000 may find it useful to seek advice on best practice, the qualifications available for individual service management professionals and ISO/IEC 20000 certification. Details of these can be found via the web pages in Appendix B.

Table 1 – Clause-by-clause guide to the 'Achieving ISO/IEC 20000' series

ISO/IEC 20000 clause	BIP 0030	BIP 0031	BIP 0032	BIP 0033	BIP 0034	BIP 0035	BIP 0036	BIP 0037	BIP 0038	BIP 0039
Terms and definitions	X									X
Management responsibility	X								X	X
Documentation requirements		X								X
Competence, awareness and training		X								X
Planning and implementing service management									X	X
Plan – Do – Check – Act cycle									X	X
Planning and implementing new or changed services									X	X
Service level management				X						X
Service reporting			X							X
Service continuity and availability management							X			X
Budgeting and accounting for IT services					X					X
Information security management	See BSI publications on information security management in the BIP 0070 series									
Capacity management								X		X
Business relationship management				X						X
Supplier management				X						X
Incident management							X			X
Problem management							X			X
Configuration management						X				X
Change management						X				X
Release management						X				X

Chapter 1

ISO/IEC 20000 fundamentals

What is integrated service management?

The introduction to ISO/IEC 20000-1 states the following:

> 'This part of ISO/IEC 20000 promotes the adoption of an integrated process approach to effectively deliver managed services to meet the business and customer requirements. For an organization to function effectively it has to identify and manage numerous linked activities. An activity using resources, and managed in order to enable the transformation of inputs into outputs, can be considered as a process. Often the output from one process forms an input to another.

> Co-ordinated integration and implementation of the service management processes provides the ongoing control, greater efficiency and opportunities for continual improvement.........'

Any service provider[1] aiming to achieve ISO/IEC 20000 needs to understand what is meant by 'integrated service management' and what benefits it delivers. Until service management processes are integrated, the full benefits of service management will not be achieved. The full benefits are only obtained when information and control flows from one process to another in a way that is understood and predictable.

Processes implemented in isolation are immature and unsophisticated. In contrast, integrated processes are mature and enable the service provider to optimize service management and align the services with the business needs.

Depending on the individual service provider's circumstances, some service management processes in the scope of ISO/IEC 20000 need information from every other process at some time. Conversely, some service management processes provide information that may be used by every other process. As described in Chapter 2, the flow of information

---

[1] The service provider is the organization that is aiming to achieve ISO/IEC 20000.

between one process and another may be direct or it may be via other processes, according to the individual circumstances of the service provider. Although integration of service management is a sign of excellence in the service provider's approach, there is no single way of integrating processes.

Integrated service management results from the use of many best practices, which can include:

- overall control by the management system;
- effective service management planning;
- accountability for the service management plan;
- agreed policies and service management objectives;
- processes that reflect business needs;
- clarity on the scope and ownership of each process;
- processes that underpin policies and deliver against service management objectives;
- understanding of process interfaces;
- information flows between processes, as metrics and service reports;
- policies, processes and procedures that can be measured;
- documents and records that are current and controlled;
- staff with clear roles and responsibilities and the correct skills;
- effective use of service management tools.

What is a process interface?

ISO/IEC 20000 uses the term 'process' to mean an activity using resources to transform inputs to outputs. Each process should have a clearly defined scope. A process interface is the boundary of the process.

Process integration is the linking of processes by the flow of information between processes.

Integration of processes may be as simple as the end of one process interfacing with the start of another. In practice, mapping out the interfaces and how they are integrated usually shows a complex set of relationships with multiple branches (such as shown in Figure 1). Interfacing may be via shared data stores, which has the benefit of multiple processes being lined to the same information source. More examples are provided in Chapter 2.

To integrate processes, the interfaces need to be understood and documented, particularly where the relationships between integrated processes are complex.

The relationships between policy, process and procedure for service management is also important in defining interfaces and integrating processes and are described in more detail in Chapter 3.

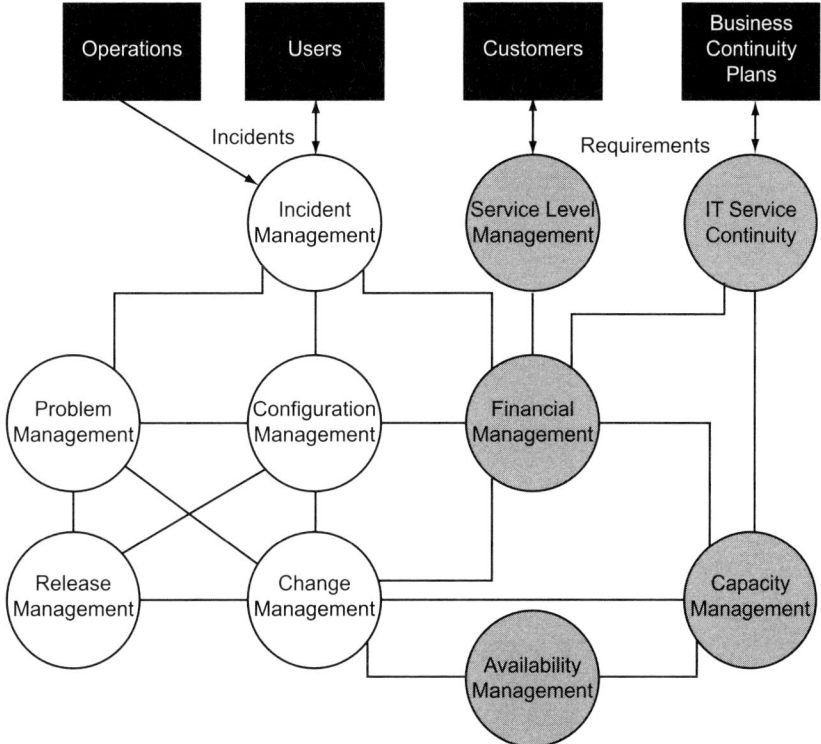

Figure 1 – Example process interface

Process, people and technology

The integration of processes has to take into account not only the individual processes and their interfaces, but also the people and technology required for effective service management. ISO/IEC 20000-1, 3.3 requires management to be actively involved in the development of competence, awareness and training in service management. This topic is described in BIP 0031, *Why people matter.*

As a process-based standard, ISO/IEC 20000 does not specify requirements for tools. Understanding the scale and nature of automation that is possible and cost-effective is also important to the overall owner of service management, the process owners of the individual processes and those involved in service improvement and service reporting. Process ownership is described in more detail in Chapter 3. Service and process improvements are described in Chapters 5 to 8.

Management commitment

ISO/IEC 20000 is a management system standard that specifies requirements for management responsibilities, effective planning for service management, full integration of the Plan-Do-Check-Act (PDCA) cycle and service management processes. The results of this are:

- a well-understood scope for service management;
- the ability to handle major changes;
- delivery of continuing service improvements.

Without management commitment, processes evolve into parochial activities, potentially conflicting and competing for resources. Management responsibilities are described in Chapter 3.

Planning service management

The service management plan

ISO/IEC 20000-1 requires that there is a service management plan that:

'.... defines the interfaces between processes and the manner in which the activities of those processes are to be coordinated ...'.

Implementing and improving service management, the requirements for the PDCA cycle and planning for new and changed services are all very closely linked. The PDCA cycle is described in Chapters 4 to 8.

The PDCA cycle starts with the 'Plan' stage, as described in Chapter 5. The Plan is implemented in the 'Do' stage, described in Chapter 6. Input is provided by the 'Check' stage of the PDCA cycle, described in Chapter 7. Improvements are made in the 'Act' stage, described in Chapter 8.

Phased implementation

Many service providers introduce service management in phases, as described in Chapter 5. Integration of processes is an important consideration when this approach is adopted as integration may be affected by each phase of new or changed processes.

New or changed services

It is also particularly important to service management that once processes are in place they are able to accommodate planning for new and changed services. This is covered by clause 5 of ISO/IEC 20000-1 and is described in Chapter 9.

CHAPTER 2

Process integration

Introduction

One of the main reasons for the publication of ISO/IEC 20000 was to promote an integrated approach to service management, as described in the opening sentence of the introduction to ISO/IEC 20000-1.

Establishing the changes required to the working culture that would bring about collaborative working between process owners, other managers and senior management, staff and different teams is vital to integrating service management processes. Integrated processes may be designed, documented, implemented and initially supported, but fail as people readopt parochial views of their roles and the role of their colleagues. Technology intended for the use of a single group of staff or for a single process may be inadequate for the support of integrated processes, where integration is primarily the flow of information across process and organizational boundaries.

Integrating processes, changing the culture and adopting technology may be one of the biggest challenges facing a service provider. Integration also brings some of the biggest benefits, such as reduced costs, tasks completed in less time, increased service levels and increased satisfaction for customers, employees and shareholders. Process integration also enhances the ability of a service provider to adapt as the changing needs of customer and market become apparent.

This chapter describes what is meant by integration, the reasons why it is so important and several examples of process integration. Additional examples of metrics are included in the final section of this chapter.

What is integration?

Integrated and managed interfaces are characterized by a demonstrable understanding of:

- the policies that apply to the processes and to the management of interfaces between processes;

- the scope and limits of each process;
- the responsibilities of those involved in each process;
- the information provided by each process that flows from one process to another, who produces it and how it is used.

Evidence of how interfaces between processes are managed is required for an ISO/IEC 20000 audit. This involves demonstrating an understanding of roles, responsibilities and information, such as service reports, produced by one process but used in another.

The examples in this chapter show some of the information flows that are important for process integration. For the sake of simplicity, the figures in this chapter show only the most important interfaces between the processes and to the overall planning.

Flow of information and control

A consistent approach for managing and controlling service and infrastructure changes increases efficiency, and establishes clear accountability and traceability as the services and infrastructure evolve. Exactly what information flows between processes is dependent on a service provider's particular circumstances, the policies that the processes underpin and on the actual detail of procedures.

It must be clear at what point control of events passes between processes. For example, if the customer is planning a major change to their business activities, how is this information passed from business relationship management to service level management and from service level management to supplier management? Who controls what decisions on service level agreement (SLA) targets and the supplier's contractual commitments, should they need to change as a result of the customer's new business plans? Information on this must flow from the business relationship and service level management processes to the supplier management process.

An auditor will assess the service provider's understanding of the process interfaces and how effective the flow of information and control is between the processes. An auditor will expect to see evidence of an integrated approach to planning and implementing the processes based on the requirements in ISO/IEC 20000-1.

Checklist 1 illustrates the type of information that an auditor will expect to see as evidence of integration. This illustration is based on the integration of the configuration, change and release management processes.

Checklist 1: Integration of control and release processes

Request for change record

- A request for change records details of the proposed change to any configuration item within a service or infrastructure.

Change scope

- Changes have a clearly defined and documented scope, i.e. the change records contain details of which configuration items are affected.

Impact assessment of change

- Configuration management provides information to the change management process on the impact of a requested change on the service and infrastructure.
- Requests for change are assessed for their impact on release plans.
- The impact of new or changed services is assessed on budgets, staff resources, existing service levels, SLAs and other targets or service commitments, service management processes, procedures, documents and records.

Verification of configuration items

- Changes to configuration items can be verified during change implementation.

Releases

- Procedures include the updating and changing of configuration information and change records including all associated updates to documentation in the release, e.g. business processes, support documents and service level agreements.
- Emergency releases are managed according to a defined process that interfaces with the emergency change management process.
- All associated updates to documentation should be included in the release, e.g. business processes, support documents and service level agreements. The impact of all new or changed configuration items required to effect the authorized changes should be assessed.

Traceability and auditability

- Changes to configuration items are traceable and auditable where appropriate.
- Release items should be traceable and secure from modification.

Reporting

- The status of configuration items, their versions, location, related changes and problems, and associated documentation are visible to those who require it.
- Change records contain details of which configuration items are affected and how they were affected by an authorized change.

Role of automation

Processes should be integrated even if each process is reliant on several information systems or tools. If the interface is manual the flow of information between processes will be limited. Under these circumstances plans for improving the flow of information should be included in the service management plan. This is particularly important where a service provider is reliant on complex supply chains, with multiple suppliers and multiple customers, as the complexity may add risks that must be carefully managed.

An auditor will expect to see evidence of the service provider's understanding of the scope of each information system or tool, how it is used to automate each process and how the processes and tools fit together, even if the interfaces are basic and manual. Figure 2 is an example of how this information may be mapped for an auditor.

Information systems and tools	3.1 Management responsibility	3.2 Documentation	3.3 Competence/awareness /training	4.1 PDCA - Plan	4.2 PDCA - Do	4.3 PDCA - Check	6.5 Capacity	6.6 Information security	7.2 Supplier	8.1 Incident	8.2 Problem	9.1 Configuration	9.2 Change	10.1 Release
Service Desk										✓	✓	✓	✓	✓
CMDB SYS1	✓	✓	✓	✓	✓	✓	✓	✓	✓	✓	✓	✓	✓	✓
CMDB SYS2									✓			✓	✓	✓
Knowledgebase							✓	✓	✓	✓	✓			
HR System	✓		✓	✓					✓			✓	✓	✓
Tool Y														✓

Figure 2 – Information systems and tools by process (illustrative)

Interface definition

Service management planning interface

Many service providers define the following information in their service management planning documents:

- terminology mapping and glossary;
- contacts;
- roles and responsibilities of those involved in each process;
- shared processes;
- process interfaces where the supplier uses a different process or tool to the service provider;
- information provided by each process at an organizational boundary; by whom and when it is produced;
- shared data and information;
- service level measures that apply across their supply chain.

Documenting the inputs and outputs for a process

It is advisable to keep track of the interfaces between processes and an auditor will find the information of interest. Tables 2 and 3 are illustrations of how a service provider may document the information input to and output from processes. Table 2 shows examples of inputs, and Table 3 shows examples of outputs to and from the availability management process.

Alternative methods of showing interfaces

Another method of defining the information flows between processes is to identify both the input and the **source** of input. This may be a role, another process and/or a tool. The output from the controlling process is identified together with the role, process and/or tool that receives the output information.

Examples are given in Table 4 to illustrate a type of useful record. However, the inexperienced reader may become confused by assuming that input and output are directly linked if they are on the same row. Care needs to be taken to avoid giving this impression when it is not true.

When planning the implementation of best practice service management it will be advisable to keep track of the most important interfaces between processes. A few examples are given in Table 4 to illustrate a form of useful record. Visualization also promotes effective communication and collaboration on process improvements.

Table 2 – Example inputs for availability management

Input from	Information	ISO/IEC 20000 objective or requirement
Service level management	Availability requirements	Availability ......requirements shall be identified on the basis of ....SLAs ....
Service continuity management	Business critical services and business impact of unavailability	To ensure that agreed obligations to customers can be met
Service level management	Availability requirements	Availability .... plans shall be maintained to ensure that they reflect agreed changes required by the business
Change management	Request for impact assessment on availability management and availability plan	The change management process shall assess the impact of any change on the availability .... plan
Incident management	Incident data, major incidents and outages	Unplanned non-availability shall be investigated ....
Problem management	Root cause of incidents that cause or may cause downtime	
Configuration management	Components that make up a service to enable component failure impact analysis to be performed	To ensure that agreed obligations to customers can be met in all circumstances
PDCA	Audit report	

Table 3 – Example outputs from availability management

Output to	Information	ISO/IEC 20000 requirement
Service reporting	Availability metrics	Availability shall be measured and recorded
Change management	Impact assessment of proposed changes on the availability plan	The change management process shall assess the impact of any change on the availability ... plan
A plan for improving the service	Changes to improve availability	Unplanned non-availability shall be investigated and appropriate actions taken
Change management	Proposed changes required for availability management	Unplanned non-availability shall be investigated and appropriate actions taken

Table 4 – Example interface definition

Input information	Source of input	Process	Output of information	Output to
Supplier service report of major incident	Supplier and the service provider's supplier management	Service level management	Impact statement on customer's service	Customer, business relationship management and supplier management
			Recommendations on implications for the supplier's contract	Supplier management
Customer's business plans	Customer and/or stakeholders	Business relationship management	Implications of major changes on service and service levels	Service level management
Implications of major changes on service and service levels	Business relationship management	Service level management	Discussion document on proposed changes to the services, SLAs and service catalogue	Business relationship management and customers/stakeholders
Customer satisfaction feedback	Customer, stakeholders, end users	Business relationship management	Analysis of the strengths and weakness of the service	Service level management
			Recommendations for improvements	PDCA cycle/service improvement
Details of change to subcontracted supplier	Lead supplier	Supplier management	Update for the service catalogue	Service level management
			Assessment of the impact on the customer's service	Service level management

Example interfaces

Relationship management

To enable business and service changes to be effectively managed, many processes rely on the relationship management processes to obtain information on business and supplier changes that may impact the service provider and customer's plans. This is described in more detail in BIP 0033, *Managing end-to-end service.*

Business relationship management
ISO/IEC 20000-1 requires that the business relationship management process includes a mechanism for ensuring the service provider remains aware of changes in business needs, and any major changes that are being planned by the customer. This requires the business relationship management process to be integrated with other processes. An auditor may seek evidence of how past changes to the business and customer requirements were managed, as a test of how well the process has worked in practice.

Supplier management
ISO/IEC 20000-1 includes a requirement that: '*The interfaces between processes used by each party shall be documented and agreed.*'
An auditor will expect the interfaces for all processes that cross organizational boundaries to be defined and understood. It is also important that there is a defined approach to the managing and use of configuration items that are shared with the customer or supplier, e.g. a logging system or infrastructure.

It is the service provider's responsibility to decide what is required of suppliers and to agree the extent that the processes may be tailored to the supplier's environment. These requirements are passed formally to the supplier via the supplier management process.

It is also advisable for service management processes to reflect the relationships between lead suppliers and the lead supplier's own suppliers (i.e. subcontracted suppliers). As described in BIP 0033, *Managing end-to-end services*, the service provider does not manage subcontracted suppliers directly, but does manage suppliers and lead suppliers directly. This has implications for integration of processes. Typically, this requires service reporting by suppliers and lead suppliers. Lead suppliers normally report on the whole service they manage, including the contribution of each of their subcontractors. It is also advisable for the service provider to check that their supplier and lead suppliers continue to follow the agreed processes and procedures.

Service level management

Major business changes, e.g. business reorganizations, mergers and changing customer requirements, can require the service level management process to adjust, redefine or temporarily suspend service level commitments. Good configuration management of the services enables the service level management process to be responsive to customer's business needs.

Where there are changes to either the range of services, the level of service, performance or workload volumes or types, this is reflected in amendments to the SLA that will be managed through the change management process. Changes to the SLA may require changes to supporting agreements such as OLA[2]s and this may also ripple through to one or more of the services provided by suppliers.

This may require changes to contracts between the service provider and suppliers, under contract change control procedures. In this example, the managers responsible for business relationship management, service level management and supplier management would be involved in the assessment, implementation and review of the change for each aspect of the service and for each process.

An auditor will expect to see evidence of how service level management deliverables are changed in a controlled manner. There would normally be implications for other service management processes as they may be involved in impact assessment and the implementation of changes to their processes.

Incident and problem management

Operational changes are required on an ongoing basis to fix problems and known errors. The configuration management process enables effective and efficient incident and problem management as it supports the easy recording of diagnostic information on the affected configuration items. For example, a support person may simply find the affected asset tag from a shortlist of assets owned by a user rather than have to describe the asset details in text.

The problem management process depends on good configuration information to determine the root cause of incidents. When the problem management process identifies the known error, the actual configuration item that is causing the problem is identified in configuration management. The problem management process raises a request for change to fix the known error.

---

[2] Operational level agreement is a common term for a document(s) that describes each internal support group's contribution to the overall service.

As shown in the example in Figure 3 an event is received by the incident management process and the initial diagnosis indicates there is a link between the event and a CI. For example, a desktop application or an item of hardware. In this example there is no workaround so the problem management process investigates the cause and identifies other CIs that are also affected. When the problem management process identifies a known error, the actual configuration management process raises a request for a change to fix the known error. The fix is incorporated into a release and on completion the problem management process will provide feedback on the success or failure of the change (i.e. did it fix the error?).

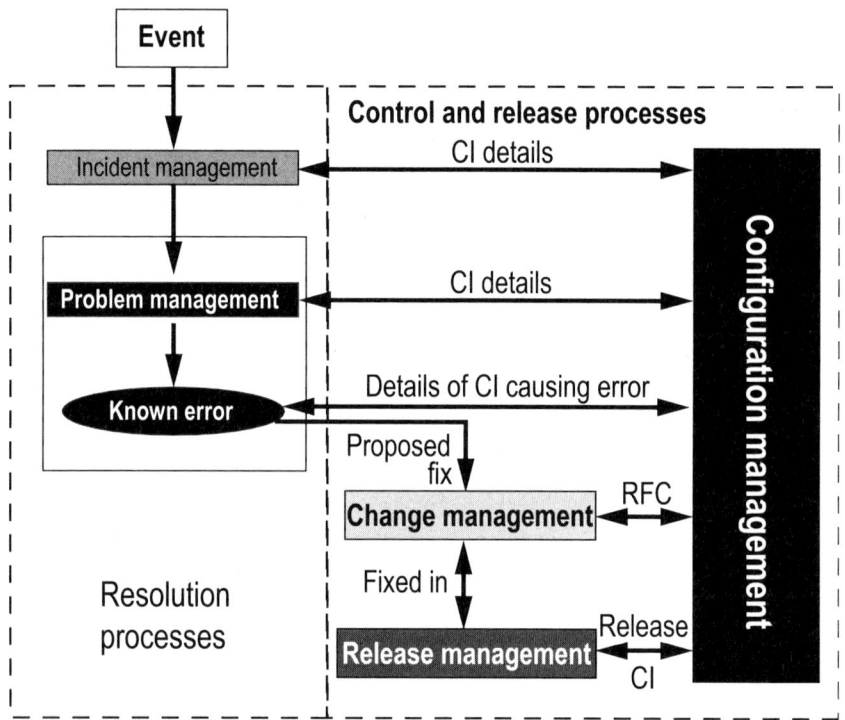

Figure 3 – Resolution, control and release process interfaces

Like other examples of integrated processes there could be a number of effective and acceptable permutations.

Proactive problem management ensures that problems and known errors are linked to the changes or configuration items that caused the problem. This assists with analysis of problems. An auditor will seek evidence on how changes and releases impact the number and type of incidents and problems. This is also described in BIP 0035, *Enabling change* and BIP 0036, *Keeping the service going.*

Information security management

Although information security management is not described in any detail in the 'Achieving ISO/IEC 20000' series as there are already appropriate BSI publications on security, as listed in Appendix B, security does have many important interfaces with the management system requirements and the other service management processes.

As described in the example *A policy by another name* in Chapter 3, in order to implement this security management policy and procedures requires integration of the security management process with the overall management process (i.e. the management system requirements, including those that relate to competence, awareness and training in ISO/IEC 20000-1, 3.3).

Using the policy (referred to by the organization as 'The Security Standard') as an example, the interfaces between the security management policy and process and some of the other processes are shown in Figures 4 and 5.

In Figure 4, these interfaces relate to a security policy that states that

> *'It is essential that all staff understand and comply with those aspects of the security standard that relate to protecting the integrity of information and prevention of unauthorized access,'*

and that

> *'Each manager is accountable for ensuring that their staff are aware of and understand the company's security standard and the role they personally play in ensuring the standard is complied with,'*

as described in the example *A policy by another name* in Chapter 3.

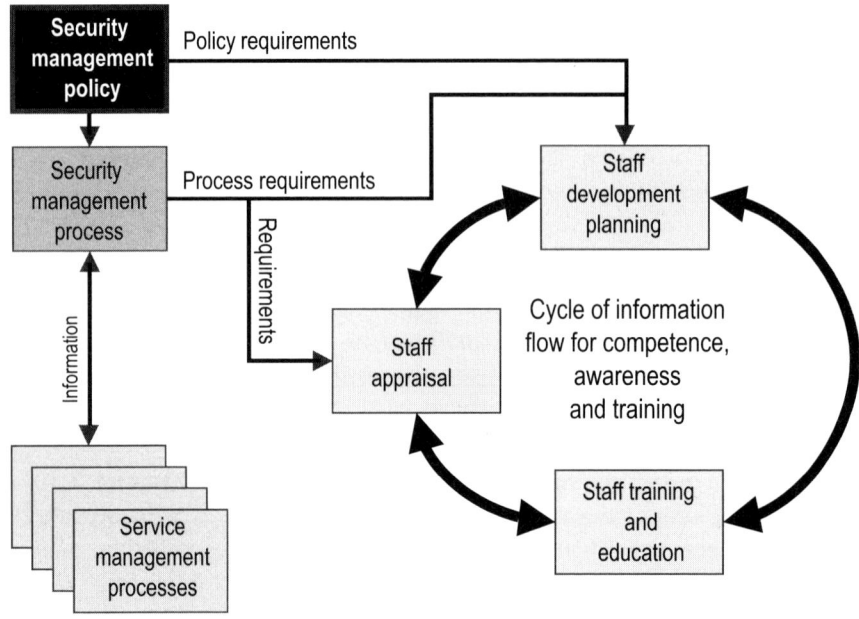

Figure 4 – Security interfaces and management processes

In Figure 5, the interfaces relate to the part of a security policy that states:

'.....*staff are required to:*

- *report immediately any actual or suspected security breach or unauthorized access attempt to the IT infrastructure and related materials;*

- *record using the incident management process all suspected and actual security events immediately, and with all the required details;*

- *escalate all level 1 security events to the management team;*

- *provide...weekly reports on the numbers, types and trends in security events will be issued to the CEO and in the absence of the CEO, to the Finance Director;*

- *change management process will be used to correct all security breaches,'*

as described in *A policy by another name* in Chapter 3.

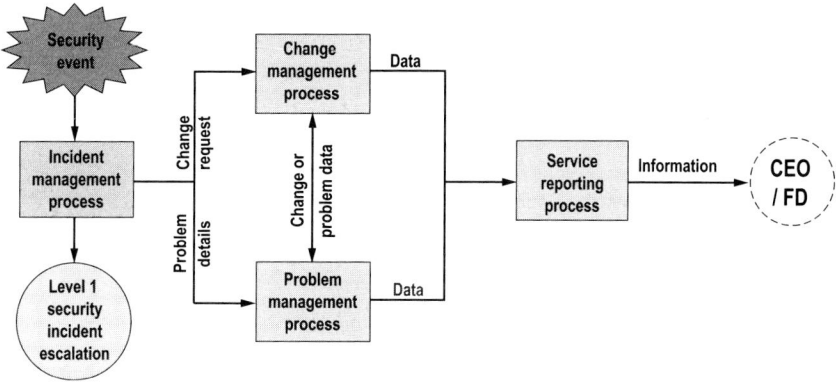

Figure 5 – Security interfaces and service management processes

Budgeting and accounting interfaces

Changes to financial policies and procedures impact other service management processes and decision making. It will also require review and revision of financial reports. Failure to do so may adversely affect the visibility and control over costs and risks, due to the ineffective integration of processes.

Examples of interfaces to the budgeting and accounting processes that are referred to briefly in BIP 0034, *Finance for service managers* are described in more detail below.

Changes to service
Any new or changed service or even a straightforward change to the technology used to deliver the service incurs a cost. This type of change may be small, for example the time costs of granting or removing access rights, or may be a major technology 'refresh programme', a widespread change to business processes or the introduction of a new service. ISO/IEC 20000-1 requires the cost to be considered for each of these changes.

For routine and simple changes costs are not normally calculated each time. Instead an agreed nominal cost is used in the budget and accounting processes. It is also used when planning resources, such as staff to grant or remove access rights. Other uses are for baselines and in predictions of what will be required following a change, as part of the capacity management process.

There is a requirement that 'plans for new or changed services shall consider the cost impact', so that implementation plans are the product of management decisions based on an understanding of expected costs.

Configuration management information

The interface between the configuration management process and financial asset accounting process provides information that can be used for the financial management of assets. Information on the number and types of each asset may flow to the budgeting and accounting processes for use in drawing up accounts, balance sheets and budgets for next year (see Figure 6).

Deficiencies in the configuration management process may mean that assets are 'lost' or are recorded as being held when they have been disposed of. Some assets, such as PCs and printers, are notoriously difficult to keep track of by any process as they are relatively easily moved, changed or misplaced by users or the service provider's own staff. Usually the person involved does not realize that these actions have serious implications for configuration management information and its use by the budgeting and accounting processes at the very least. Small items are also relatively easily stolen.

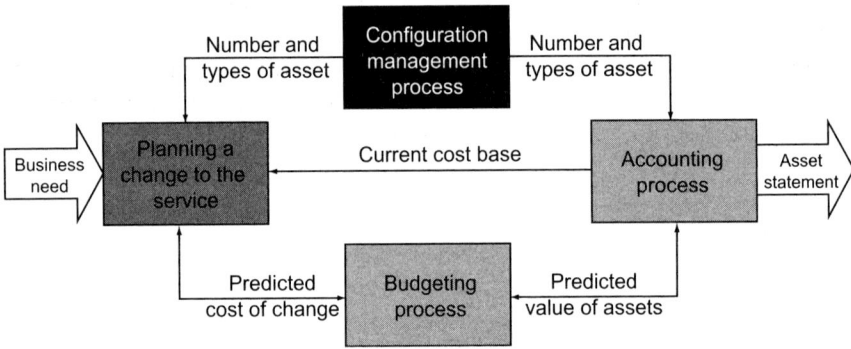

Figure 6 – Financial and configuration management processes

Sometimes deficiencies in configuration management information and associated financial records are not known about until the charges, costs or even the balance sheet itself, is challenged and the numbers and types of assets are checked – often by a slow and expensive physical audit.

Unit costs

One of the most useful benefits of a high standard of service management, and in particular of a high standard of financial management processes, is that value for money of the current service can be measured and the financial benefits of improvements and other changes can be predicted. It becomes possible to check how accurate the prediction of financial benefits was, and to learn lessons on how to make more accurate predictions in the future.

Service and process improvements are often designed to reduce costs and increase value for money. For example, a technology refresh programme may incur very large capital costs initially, but then the benefit is provided by reduced service failures, cheaper support and less disruption of the customer's business activities. For this to work effectively, the information on costs may have to flow to and from the financial processes to every other process, either directly or indirectly. This requires the scope of each process to be understood, the interfaces to be defined and for the information to flow between processes in a controlled and predictable manner.

The process map for this level of process integration will inevitably be complex, but metrics showing the end results may be relatively simple as they are the result of aggregation of information from many processes. By showing metrics such as the unit cost of incident and problem solving changing over time, it is possible to measure the benefits of changes targeted at making resolution more efficient.

An example of a metric that can be used to show the aggregated effect of many changes, such as from a technology refresh or process re-engineering programme, is shown in Figure 7. This example is based on the experience of a service provider that made three phases of changes. The three phases all covered improvements in service management processes and improvements in the reliability of the technology.

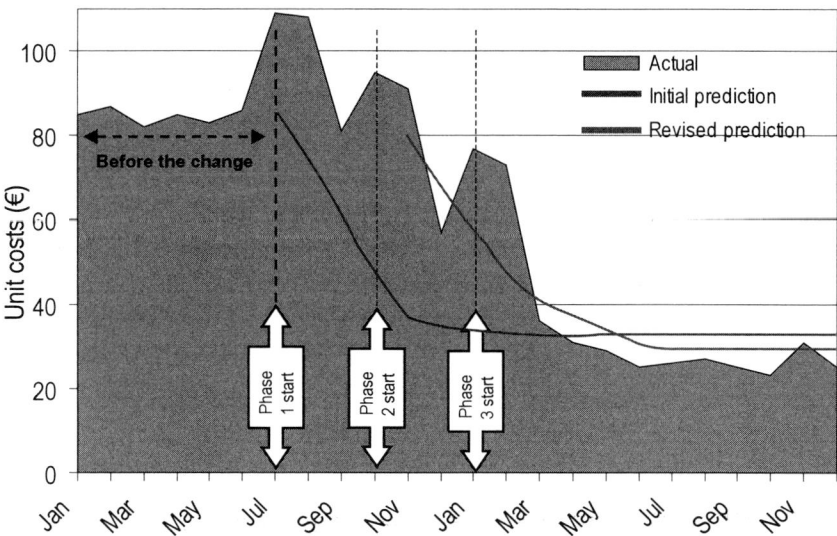

Figure 7 – Unit cost of incident and problem solving

Improvements were made to the change, configuration, release, availability, incident and problem management processes. The total effect of improvements to so many processes was difficult to predict and the first prediction (shown by the solid blue line in Figure 7) was too optimistic, particularly for phase 1 and the early part of phase 2. Because the predictions were wrong the assumptions were checked.

With the benefit of data from the first phase and part of the second phase, a second prediction was made. This was more cautious and was eventually found to be much more accurate than the first prediction. The information shown in Figure 7 was based on data from many processes, aggregated to show the cost-benefit of the changes overall.

Assessment of suppliers
Financial information is used to select a supplier and judge the value for money of the services they provide, e.g. compared to the same service from another supplier or from an in-house team.

Service reporting

Service reports are a key part of information flow between processes, and therefore of integration of processes. Plans to change a process must not be implemented unless the impact of the planned change on service reporting and the use of service reports by other processes has been considered, is understood and is acceptable for service management overall.

Capacity Planning

Many service providers subsume aspects of capacity management into the PDCA cycle, so the interface between the capacity management process and the PDCA cycle varies from one service provider to another. Two possible approaches are illustrated in Figures 8 and 9.

Improvements via the PDCA cycle
One approach is to incorporate all capacity management checks and the implementation of identified process improvements into the PDCA cycle. With this approach there is no review of efficiency or planning for process improvements done within the capacity management process.

This leaves many aspects of the capacity management process within the direct control of the capacity management process. For example, production of the capacity management plan tuning of service performance and provision of adequate capacity and performance.

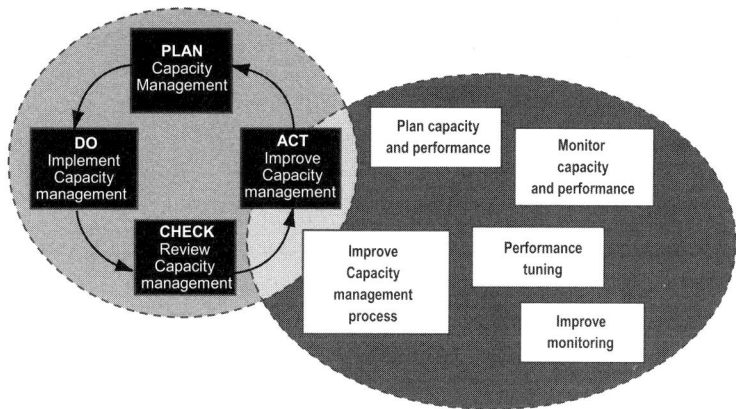

Figure 8 – Improvements via the PDCA cycle

Interface to the PDCA cycle

Another approach is for all aspects of the capacity management process, including process improvements to be done within the capacity management process itself. This means that all the ISO/IEC 20000 requirements for continuing improvements and day-to-day capacity management are under the direct and local control of the capacity management process. The capacity management process then interfaces to the overall PDCA cycle so that there is a view of service management as a whole for the process owners and other responsible managers, as shown in Figure 9.

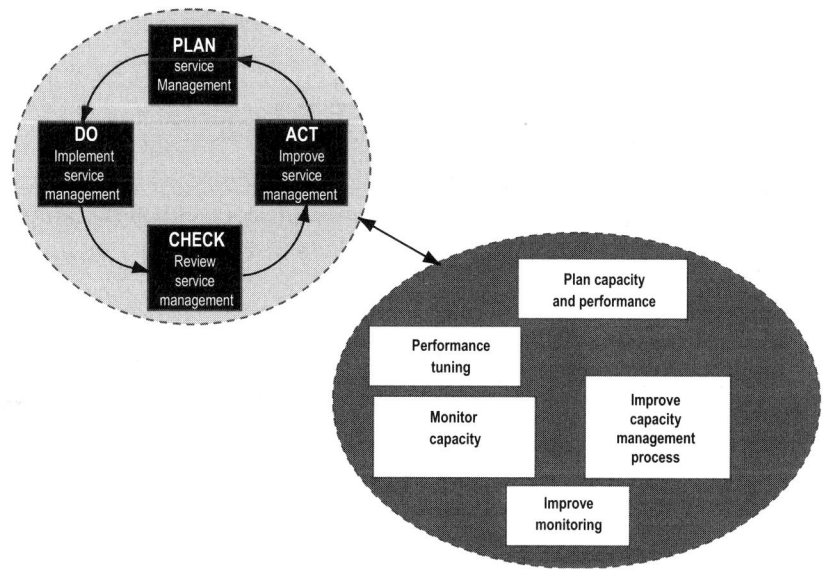

Figure 9 – Localized improvements

Service providers may find it more effective to incorporate the more proactive aspects of service management processes into the PDCA cycle, as described above for the capacity management process. Others may consider it more effective to keep all reactive and proactive aspects of each service management process locally and in the process itself, with only an interface to the PDCA cycle, so that the PDCA cycle retains overall control. This is largely an organizational issue.

Whichever approach is adopted by the service provider there must be clarity on roles and responsibilities and who is accountable, responsible, consulted and informed for each process. All ISO/IEC 20000 requirements for each process, for planning and for day-to-day activities must be met.

Managing integrated changes

To manage frequent changes successfully, the management team needs to understand the framework of measurements and controls involved in achieving ISO/IEC 20000. An example high-level framework is described in Chapter 3, and illustrated in Figure 11.

It is important that the interfaces between the processes are aligned during and after changes that may be made to the framework and documentation. For example, adding a new type of configuration item may affect the change impact assessment procedure, configuration status reporting, the service report for measuring the success or failure of changes to different configuration item types and related training deliverables. Similarly a change to the SLA may have implications for every other process, including the processes covered by the management system responsibilities and the supplier management process.

Example metrics and audit evidence

The examples shown in Tables 5 and 6 are only illustrations as each service provider may meet the requirements of ISO/IEC 20000 by using different metrics.

Table 5 – Example metric on process integration

Metric	Type of metric	Purpose and ISO/IEC 20000 objective
Integration	Process maps or Tables such as Tables 2 to 4	The plans shall at a minimum define........the interfaces between service management processes and the manner in which the activities are to be co-ordinated

Evidence on the effectiveness of a process should not be produced specifically for an audit. What evidence is necessary is left to the judgment of the individual auditor but typical examples are illustrated below.

As a minimum the auditor will expect to see evidence of the effectiveness of each requirement, i.e. evidence that supports how each service provider meets the requirements shown by the use of '**shall**', and that effectiveness has been sustained for a suitable period of time.

It is not possible to develop a list of audit evidence against the requirements in ISO/IEC 20000-1 that applies equally to all service providers. Each service provider's processes and procedures may meet the requirements but differ at the detailed level. As a consequence differences in audit evidence will occur across different service providers.

Table 6 – Example audit evidence for requirements

Objective and requirement	Example audit evidence
All service management objectives are relevant to process integration, but in particular those of the PDCA cycle, i.e. Objective: To plan the implementation and delivery of service management.	
Service management **shall** be planned. The plans **shall** at a minimum define........the interfaces between service management processes and the manner in which the activities are to be co-ordinated	Interface maps showing inputs and outputs

Chapter 3

Management commitment

Introduction

This chapter describes the importance of a service provider's management commitment to best practice service management and how this is reflected in the requirements of ISO/IEC 20000-1.

This chapter focuses on the management system requirements in clauses 3.1 and 3.3 and on the management commitment aspects of clause 4 of ISO/IEC 20000-1. These clauses reflect the role of ISO/IEC 20000 as a management system standard.

Clause 3, *Requirements for a management system* has the overall objective:

> *'To provide a management system, including policies and a framework to enable the effective management and implementation of all IT services.'*

This objective covers:

- management responsibilities, (3.1);
- documentation requirements, (3.2; see BIP 0030, *Management decisions and documentation*);
- competence, awareness and training commitment, (3.3).

The requirements for competence, awareness and training are also described in more detail in BIP 0031, *Why people matter.*

Clause 4 of ISO/IEC 20000-1 contains the PDCA cycle requirements described in Chapters 4 to 8.

Management responsibilities

Many of the requirements in ISO/IEC 20000 were included so that there are explicit checks during an audit for the more common reasons that service management falls short of best practice. Some of the most common reasons are:

- lack of management commitment;

- lack of process integration;
- confusion regarding what is required;
- an uncoordinated approach;
- lack of clarity on roles and responsibilities.

As a consequence, checks on accountability, responsibility and clarity on roles are a common theme in ISO/IEC 20000 requirements.

The importance of management commitment as part of achieving ISO/IEC 20000 cannot be over emphasized. This requires the service provider's senior management (described as 'top/executive management') to provide evidence of commitment to developing, implementing and improving its service management capability. For example, this may include employee excellence being recognized for implementing and upholding a programme of improvements.

The service provider's senior management must understand and demonstrate that commitment is more than signing a piece of paper. They themselves must be seen to take appropriate actions. Loss of initial enthusiasm often occurs at the same time that initial costs have been incurred, but the benefits have not yet materialized. At this time the attention of senior management may be diverted by other pressures on them and their role. Management commitment must continue to direct the ongoing improvements to service management. Adequate funds have to be allocated and kept in the budget.

A programme of improvements may be seen solely as an opportunity for individual personal advancement. Although success in improvements should help career progression, management should correct any tendency to place self-interest as the main driving factor in those involved. If short-term self-interest is allowed to dominate activities, the changes will not benefit the organization as a whole. Improvements will either take longer to establish or are less likely to be integrated. They may not even achieve what is required. Changing to a culture of collaborative working, willingness to cooperate and an interest in understanding another's perspective may be one of the biggest benefits from achieving the required integrated service management approach.

None of this happens unless it cascades down the hierarchy from senior management.

Example: The risks of isolated processes

A service provider had implemented several service management processes in a low-key programme of improvements. A new senior manager was appointed who was enthusiastic about adopting best practice service management. A review established that: there were three variants of change management; that incident management best practices were restricted to the service desk; the problem management process was limited by the poor quality of information. The only other formal process was part of the security management process, which operated in isolation.

Several 'quick hits' were implemented. These included standardizing how incidents, problems and requests were recorded and updated. This required some intensive, short-term training for all staff who recorded or updated records but quickly provided information for the problem management process.

There were some difficulties in rationalizing the variants in the change management process, partly due to the almost complete absence of configuration information. A plan to implement a configuration management process was agreed. This included the use of a simple tool for automation of both the configuration and change management process.

The process owner for security management was also very enthusiastic. Unfortunately, the process owner failed to understand the need for integrating processes and worked diligently, but in isolation, then resisted any changes needed for integration to the rest of service management, insisting that the other processes all had to be adapted to align with the new security process. A resolution for this conflict was being sought when a virus affected the whole service. The impact was much worse because the incident was not recorded by the incident management process and not recognized as a threat until much damage had been done.

Key point:

All the process owners recognized that they needed to agree an approach to integration quickly and that the conflicting views must not cause a delay. Defining the scope of each process and how they should be integrated was recognized as essential to the whole of service management.

Top-down approach

Process integration is inherently easier if approached 'top-down'. The top-down approach starts with agreement on the objectives and policies for service management, mapping to the scope of ISO/IEC 20000-1. Development of plans is described in detail in Chapter 5.

ISO/IEC 20000-1 requires that the objectives of service management are understood, align with the policies and are supported by senior management. The objectives provide tangible details of how policies are to be delivered, often including dates, times and specific deliverables. The dates, times or specific deliverables can be incorporated in the service management plan(s). The combination of policies and objectives give clear management direction and goals to those involved in the management processes and procedures.

The top-down approach, illustrated in Figure 10, shows the relationship between management responsibilities (ISO/IEC 20000-1, 3), policies and objectives for service management, the PDCA cycle and the requirements for planning and implementing new or changed services. The top-down approach results in integrated processes supported by a cohesive and logical set of service management procedures.

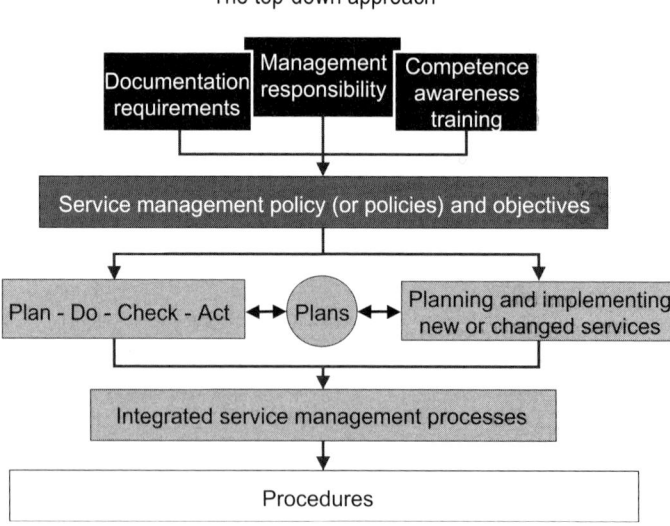

Figure 10 – The top-down approach

Policies, objectives and plans must all reflect the agreed scope of the overall service management as well as the scope of each individual process. The scope of a process is described in Chapter 5.

Example: Service improvement objective

To ensure that within 12 months the service is functioning as planned, implemented effectively and that the working environment conforms to applicable documentation.

 ## Example: Service improvement policy

The service improvement programme shall improve the quality, reliability, efficiency and effectiveness of the service provided to meet agreed service targets. Records must be maintained with details of incidents, problems and changes and used to identify service improvements.

Management commitment and a top-down approach to service management planning are also important in ensuring that there is a logical relationship between policy, process and procedure, as described in the section *Policy, process and procedure* later in this chapter.

During an audit, the service provider must be able to demonstrate that policies both define management direction and are aligned with the service management objectives.

Leadership

Communications

Implementing or improving service management is sometimes attempted without the service provider understanding how important it is to manage the change to how people work on a day-to-day basis. As a consequence, plans fail because management neither communicate the benefits, nor do they provide adequate process training, focusing only on technical training or on new service management tools.

Where a service provider is a large organization with a deep hierarchy of staff based in a large number of separate locations, communications, cascading management intentions, is difficult. Management intentions at senior levels dissipate as they cascade down the hierarchy, so that junior members may either not hear anything at all or get a confused message. When this is the case it is even more important that communication and cascading of management intentions are done well. This normally requires more positive action and resources than is normally required for a small organization where everyone knows each other and they all are located close together. The topic of communications is also described in BIP 0031, *Why people matter*.

Grass-roots support

There are many advantages to a top-down approach combined with a safety net of bottom-up support from local enthusiasts acting as agents of change. It is important and part of good senior management practice to recognize the energy and influence of more junior management and practitioners. Strong communities of enthusiasts cannot offset the effects of bad or non-existent leadership, but they can do much to redeem some of the failings of weak leadership.

It is often junior enthusiasts that initiate new ideas and identify practical approaches because of their detailed understanding of day-to-day service. Once a sizeable community of best practice enthusiasts is established, management can no longer be vague or tentative with their statements and policies. Only a naive manager attempts to manage the scale of change required without the support and cooperation of more junior colleagues.

Example: The benefits of good leadership

A commercial service provider recruited a manager with a track record in implementing service management. This was important as the service provider had to achieve ISO/IEC 20000 in 15 months.

The new manager was responsible for introducing new processes and the improvements to those already in place. The first stage went well, improving incident and problem management processes. Change management was improved by access to configuration information.

The service provider's CEO attended a meeting with a customer, who demanded an urgent change needed for a new product. This had not been raised before and was needed in three days. In the past short notice requests had resulted in badly implemented changes that had affected the service for many weeks.

The agreed they would use the emergency change procedure. This was preferable to not using the change management process at all. The emergency change procedure involved a rapid risk assessment by several highly skilled people pulled from other tasks. The emergency change was implemented at the time requested, but an important scheduled change could not be done as it conflicted with the emergency change.

The service provider discussed this conflict with the customer and got agreement to which had priority. Afterwards, they were able to explain the direct, indirect and opportunity costs of having to use the emergency change process and the delay of the scheduled change.

Although reluctant to accept that the short notice had created so many difficulties the cost information was convincing. The customer agreed to discuss business plans with the manager responsible for the relationship between the customer and the service provider, and do this with more notice.

Key point:

The CEO demonstrated support for service management best practices. The events brought new understanding of the benefits of change management and business relationship management.

Business needs and customer satisfaction

What does the customer want?

Service management planning must be based on an understanding of the customer's business needs and what will improve customer satisfaction. What is important to the customer will be invaluable in identifying not only what needs to be done, but the order and priority of improvement. The customer's views on what is required may be very different to the views of the service provider, particularly when processes are absent or have major deficiencies.

Information on the customer's strategy should also be collected and used to align the strategy of the customer's organization with that of the service provider.

Sources of information

Information on business needs and views on the existing service may be obtained from a number of sources. For example, information can be obtained by discussions with the customer and from satisfaction surveys. This is described in more detail in BIP 0033, *Managing end-to-end services*. The service provider may also do market research. This is particularly relevant where the service provider is a provider of consumer services, i.e. a service with many individual customers, e.g. an internet service provider or a telecommunications service provider.

Although there are many sources of information on business needs, collecting the information should not be based on a free-for-all activity with every process collecting information haphazardly. A haphazard approach introduces increased errors and gaps in knowledge. Collecting of information should be linked to a specific need, such as development of policies and processes. Scoping each process so that it is clear which process collects what information and when it should be collected is an important part of integrated service management.

The information on the customer's business needs may be collected by more than one process and used by more than one process. For some, such as the capacity, service continuity and availability management processes, an understanding of the customer's business needs is used for the management of risk to the services.

Where the customers' business needs are not articulated, service providers need to understand the nature and dynamics of the business environment, challenges, and opportunities faced by the customers.

Common data stores

However this information is collected it is advisable for it to be controlled as a valuable resource. For example, the service level management and business relationship management processes may both collect data that should be collated and be available for use as a single logical dataset. As long as there is a clearly defined, complete, accurate and shared view of the customer's business needs, there can be multiple views or perspectives depending on the context and scope of a process. Processes using fragmented sources of data quickly become misaligned as each process is operating on a different basis.

Converting into service management plans

The process for translating customers' requirements into senior management intentions as policies, objectives and service management plans and the actual services is part of the planning process described in Chapter 5.

Example: Parochial, short-sighted planning

A service provider had done *ad hoc* implementation of service management, starting with basic incident and change management processes. As a start to implementing more processes a workshop was run for the management team. Although only two managers had any training or experience in best practice service management it was believed that they understood what was needed and should agree priorities for implementing service management. There had been a number of security incidents, a security alert and a flood, all of which had resulted in lost service.

As a result of the recent events, the managers decided that they should give high priority to the information security management, IT service continuity, availability and change management processes.

There was only rudimentary service level management, with no service level agreements. The concept of business relationship management was not understood.

The improvements from processes that were implemented were limited and slow. As there were no major incidents relating to security or service continuity in the months after the work started, so these processes were not visible to the customer.

After many complaints were received about the service not reflecting the needs of the customer's business, a series of meetings were held and it was recognized that improvements should take the customer's needs and concerns into account. This resulted in the implementation of the business relationship management process. This in turn provided useful information on the customer's business needs, for service management planning.

Key point:

The importance of the business relationship management and service level management processes, with information on the customer's business strategy, plans and on general sector knowledge, allowed the service provider to rescue the service management plan just as it was about to fail.

Management coordination

ISO/IEC 20000-1 includes a requirement that a member of the management team is identified as being responsible for the coordination and management of all services. This is described in the section on the *Senior responsible owner*, later in this chapter.

Resourcing

Service management plans that attempt too much at once, or that are resourced with too few people, too little budget or too little management attention, do not normally succeed. Integration is particularly likely to be neglected. Management guidance is usually required to establish priorities for improvements, as a pan-organization view is required to avoid local enthusiasts giving higher priority to 'their' improvements than the benefits merit.

Managing risks

Any change carries risks that must be managed. Risks can be reduced by adopting best practice project or programme management methods for the service management plan. This is described in Chapter 5.

Additional risk management is provided by the change management process. For example, a major change to how the service is provided should be avoided when the customer's organization is also going through major changes. This could be change to the customer's business practices, new products, a time-critical business deadline or relocation. These business changes may have little or no link to the technology supported by the service provider. The service provider with good service level management and business relationship management processes will be aware of this happening.

Other risks include a new tool to automate service management processes, when the processes and procedures to be automated are not of suitable quality. The tool will not be used to its full potential and may become very unpopular.

Information is also available from the service continuity and availability management processes. These provide information on risks of non-availability and likely disasters.

Information security identifies the risks relating to security and the lack or loss of information.

Reviews

The 'Check' stage of the PDCA cycle described in Chapter 7 includes reviews of service management that check on the continuing suitability and effectiveness of the service management processes. As a process that spans all service management, the PDCA cycle identifies defects in process, not just defects in each process in isolation.

The service management framework

The documents and records are described in detail in BIP 0030, *Management decisions and documentation*.

A service management framework, such as the example shown in Figure 11, illustrates the relationships between different aspects of service management, and in particular relationship and dependencies between documents. For example:

*   training documents – may be related to the policy, process, procedure for incident management;

*   service catalogue[3] – this describes overall customer services that are partially provided under contracts with suppliers.

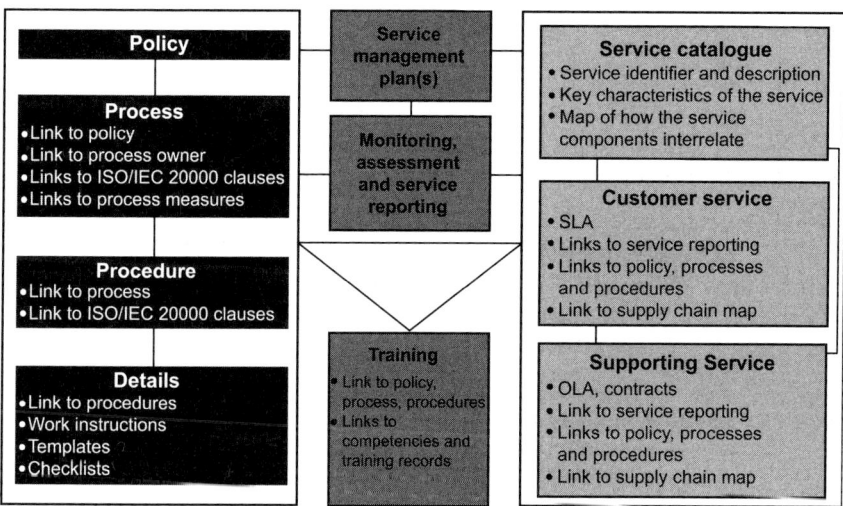

Figure 11 – Example relationships

---

[3] 'Service catalogue' is the term used in ISO/IEC 20000-2 for a respository of information on the services provided, from the customer's perspective.

Policy, process and procedure hierarchy

ISO/IEC 20000 uses the terms 'policy', 'process' and 'procedure' in the way they are used in other management system standards.

 Definition: Policy, process and procedure

'**Policy**' is the term used to describe the overall intentions and direction of a service provider, and is formally expressed by senior management.

'**Process**' is the term used to describe an activity using resources to transform inputs into outputs, i.e. 'what is to be done'.

'**Procedures**' are the specified way to carry out processes, underpinning the processes, i.e. 'how to do it'.

Policies

Policies help decisions and actions, but are not always titled 'policy'.

For example, financial standards or security 'standards' often serve the same purpose as a policy and are appropriate for meeting the policy requirements of ISO/IEC 20000-1. Some organizations adopt other terms, such as principles, business rules, standards, quality plan and governance. Use of terms other than policies is acceptable. As long as the document provides the necessary evidence of management direction, and is linked to processes and procedures as a policy should be, it does not need to be called a policy, although a standard approach to naming documents can make their use much easier. The defining characteristic is not that they are referred to as 'policies' but that they provide management direction that can be cascaded to staff.

If they are too open-ended and high level, they will not be acceptable irrespective of what name they are given. Policies should be neither vague nor generic. For example, a policy of 'we will become the best service provider' may be the basis for a useful marketing slogan, but it is useless at explaining what is to be achieved and cannot be accurately underpinned by a process.

The abstract of a 'security standard' given in the example opposite demonstrates the importance of the security management process being integrated with the other processes, such as the incident, change, continuity management and service reporting processes.

Example: A policy by another name

An organization established strict rules on security after a serious security breach had almost resulted in the closure of the organization. The rules were referred to as 'The Security Standards' and applied to the whole organization. The security standards also applied to their service provider, under the terms of the contract. Some aspects of the security standards were particularly relevant to the risks from technology and included the requirements quoted below.

It is essential that all staff understand and comply with those aspects of the security standard that relate to protecting the integrity of information and prevention of unauthorized access. The security standards are also aimed at preventing confidential information or access codes from being copied without authorization. To support this, all service provider staff are required:

- *to report immediately any actual or suspected security breach or unauthorized access attempt to the IT infrastructure and related materials;*

- *to record, using the incident management process, all suspected and actual security events immediately, and with all the required details;*

- *to escalate all level 1 security events to the management team;*

- *not to document access codes to computer systems with the exception of information recorded for continuity planning;*

- *to ensure that security information for continuity planning must only be retained in secure off-site storage, protected from damage and unauthorized access, as documented in the continuity plan.*

Weekly reports on the numbers, types and trends in security events will be issued to the CEO and in the absence of the CEO, to the Finance Director.

The change management process will be used to correct all security breaches.

Each manager is accountable for ensuring that their staff are aware of and understand the company's security standard and the role they personally play in ensuring the standard is complied with.

Key point:

The security standard serves the same purpose as the management direction provided by a policy in ISO/IEC 20000 terms. If the security standard is understood, complied with and supported by the hierarchy of process and procedures it is acceptable as a policy for an ISO/IEC 20000 audit, despite being know by a different name.

Flow of information

It is important that integration is reflected in the service provider's policies. This ensures that decisions are not based on parochial interests or influenced by conflicting views on the scope of a process that may arise between two process owners.

An audit will also check that there is a logical link between policy and process and between process and procedure. Process interfaces must also be appropriately documented and integrated.

Senior responsible owner

Which manager?

ISO/IEC 20000 refers to a 'senior responsible owner' as a manager who is both responsible and accountable for service management plans and for any service improvement activities. In addition, management commitment includes a requirement that an individual manager is identified as being responsible for the coordination and management of all services. It is common for the same manager to have responsibility for both the services and their improvements.

'Senior responsible owner' is not a job title, and for small service providers may not even be a full-time role. Many titles are used for this, such as senior service manager, service delivery manager or IT director.

When an individual is accountable, that individual must also be given suitable levels of authority in order to make decisions. This includes allocation and management of funds for service and process improvements, within the constraints of financial policies, and the overall budget available to the service provider and/or the customer. The notion of authority tightly coupled with responsibility is an important facet of management commitment.

Whatever title is used, the senior responsible owner must be actively involved in plans and improvements. Accountability also means that the success or failure of the senior responsible owner is linked to the success or failure of the processes and improvement plans.

Despite this close link, the importance ISO/IEC 20000 places on clarity of roles, responsibilities and accountabilities is not about being able to apportion blame when there are difficulties. Instead, it is about acquiring complete understanding of who does what and when, why things are done and the leadership that is required for any process to work well.

The senior responsible owner's responsibilities include recruiting appropriate staff and managing staff turnover. Staff recruitment, training, qualifications in service management and communications are described in BIP 0031, *Why people matter*. The senior responsible owner should also be a point of contact for service management, identified in escalation plans etc.

 Example: Management commitment and policies

A business set cost reduction targets after a warning about their financial position led to a drop in their share price. This cost-cutting impacted their commercial service provider, who needed to ensure that its income remained at current levels. To encourage cost reduction the customer established internal transfer of charges based on use of the service. Even minor requests had to be signed off by a manager. This led to requests being made through unofficial channels and an apparent reduction of the workload, and many requests were still made unofficially, but not logged.

The charges reduced rapidly and the relationship between the service provider and the customer became difficult.

The incident, problem and change management processes were undermined and service levels gradually degraded. Configuration management information used by the release management process became inaccurate as many small changes were made without the database being updated. After two months, a major service loss occurred after a large but low risk change. Initially, the cause could not be identified and the back out did not work. The implications for the customer's business activities were discussed by the media.

It was eventually established the 'official change' had been followed by an 'unofficial change'. The changes were made by two separate groups. The 'unofficial' change was thought to be low risk, but the two changes conflicted.

There were threats of legal action made by both parties. This was only resolved when the most senior managers of both organizations recognized that both parties needed to cooperate. It was rapidly established that the impact of the 'unofficial change' had cost over three times the short-term cost reductions.

Key point:

The customer realized that they had been unrealistic in how they could and should save costs and the service provider recognized that they were at fault in having allowed this to happen. It was agreed that it would be beneficial for both to share concerns over costs and business, to reach a compromise that would balance short- and long-term benefits and risks to both parties.

Decision-taking group

It is also recommended by ISO/IEC 20000-2 that a decision-taking group with sufficient authority to define policy and enforce its decisions supports the 'senior responsible owner'. For many service providers, this decision-taking group is made up of process owners. Process owners are described in the next section, *Process ownership*.

The auditor will also check that management commitment is real and productive, that the role of senior management, including a 'senior responsible owner', is understood, documented, unambiguous and effective.

Process ownership

Why ownership?

Process ownership is part of management commitment. One of the first steps in implementing or improving a process is to identify the process owner and allocate responsibility to that owner in the service management plans. Process ownership is also about collaboration of process owners to ensure that the processes are integrated. The consequences of not working collaboratively will be increased costs, inconsistent service, dissatisfied customers and disenchanted employees. There will be no clear direction and in the worst case it will degrade any overall strategy in relation to customers and staff.

Who are process owners?

Process owners are managers with sufficient influence to ensure processes are managed, improved and are integrated. ISO/IEC 20000 does not include any requirements related to who should have the role of process owner, or that the role is full-time or even that there is a job title 'Process Owner'. However, it is vital that a process owner is not simply a senior, distant figurehead with only nominal accountability or responsibility for the quality of a process.

Many service providers have matrix management. In matrix management individual teams are managed by service line owners, each reporting into a 'tower' or 'silo'. The process ownership is then mapped across teams so that a manager of one organizational 'silo' is responsible for an end-to-end process that involves many groups outside the line-management role. This is illustrated in Figure 12.

Grouping processes and owners

Splitting ownership of a process across more than one manager is bad practice and will not meet the requirement for there to be accountability among the management team for the quality of service management. Other than this restriction, ISO/IEC 20000 leaves the decision on allocation of process ownership to the judgment of the service provider.

Some service providers, particularly small service providers, find it best to allocate suitable groups of processes to a single manager. Some allocate process ownership to managers with operational management responsibilities for that process.

Effective grouping of processes for allocation to a single process owner is based on an understanding of several features, described below.

Scale of effort required for process implementation or improvements

If a process is new or failing badly it will require far more attention from the service provider than one that is well-established, firmly under the control of the PDCA cycle (described in Chapter 5) and which only needs to be occasionally fine-tuned for continuing improvements. Allocating more than one failing process may be unrealistic unless the processes that are being grouped are failing for the same reasons (such as lack of staff training or the need for more automation than is currently available).

Complexity of the process and organizational interfaces

A process that spans many organizational or functional boundaries requires a wider span of control and will be inherently harder to manage and improve than a process that spans only one or two boundaries. The risks of an over-extended span of control are highest when there has not been a history of collaborative working, as each group may have a different attitude to best practice service management and each may have entrenched attitudes on how the process should operate. Grouping more than two processes, each with an extended span of control may be unrealistic unless the two processes are closely related, and cross the same boundaries, so that improving one process is very similar to improving the others.

Process and personality characteristics

Many of the successful groupings are based on grouping processes that operate on similar timescales or require similar personality and behavioural characteristics. For example, combining a reactive process such as incident management with a fundamentally proactive one, such as change management, may represent a challenge to the process owner (and those people who are involved in the process operationally).

Coordination of process owners

If process ownership is allocated on a 'one process, one process owner' basis, it becomes necessary to coordinate a large group. If too many processes are allocated to individual process owners, the small group may also lack the range of personalities, experience and skills required for a successful group of decision makers.

The following groupings are relatively common:

- change and configuration management;
- problem and change management;
- service level management and business relationship management;
- IT service continuity and security;
- IT service continuity, availability and service level management.

Other combinations include incident and problem management because the two are so closely interdependent. However, if the process owner of the incident and problem management processes also has operational responsibilities, it is often found that combining the two processes under the same operational management can lead to one being neglected operationally, at the expense of the other, as the timescales over which they operate are very different. Many people find it difficult to switch between the two and many people have personalities that mean they suit one but not the other. This is described in BIP 0031, *Why people matter.*

What is an effective process owner?

If process owners have been allocated responsibility, but they have proved to be ineffective in delivering improvements, the reasons for this need to be identified and corrected or the same deficiencies may continue to affect service management in the future, however much effort is put into service improvement.

Checklist 2 illustrates some of the good features found in process owners. A process owner will improve with training by senior management or through peer group pressure. Some failings may be a fundamental part of the process owner's character and be hard to correct. A reluctant process owner is unlikely to succeed.

Checklist 2: Process owner	
Does the process owner:	
have enough seniority to exert influence?	✔
have leadership skills?	✔
actually provide leadership for improvements?	✔
…and doesn't simply pay lip-service to service management?	✔
work well with other process owners?	✔
demonstrate a holistic approach rather than a parochial attitude about 'their process'?	✔
demonstrate concern for all those involved in a process, not only people they line manage?	✔
respect the other process owners?	✔
respect the authority of the 'senior responsible owner'?	✔
understand the importance of the customer's business needs?	✔
consider more than technical issues?	✔
consider the interests of the service provider?	✔
communicate effectively to the service provider's staff?	✔

Organizational boundaries

The supply chain of multiple suppliers, the service provider, possibly several customer organizations and the complex relationship between processes means the role of process owner is particularly important in ensuring there is a flow of information and control across organizational boundaries.

Process ownership spans the full life cycle of the process, and spans all organizational units that are involved in the process. Figure 12 below does not show all processes or all departments but illustrates the principles of process ownership cutting across organizational groups.

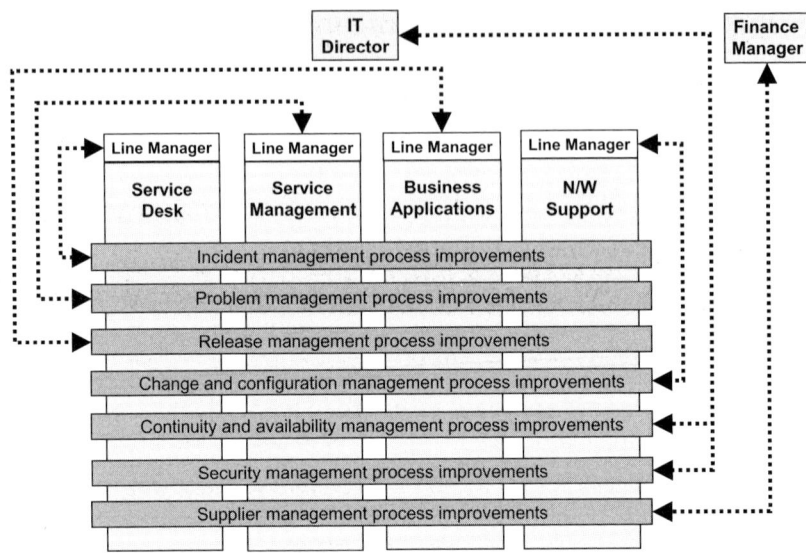

Figure 12 – Process ownership and organizational boundaries

In the example in Figure 12, which is for a small organization, there are too few managers for a single process to be allocated to a single manager, so most process owners are also line managers and several are responsible for more than one process. For example, the Service Desk Manager is the process owner for the incident management process, problem management has been allocated to the manager of the Service Management team, and the Network Support team manager is responsible for both the change and configuration management processes. The IT Director has the continuity, availability and security management processes. Supplier management has become the responsibility of the Finance Manager. All other processes are the responsibility of senior members of a specialist Service Improvement Team but are not shown, for the sake of simplicity.

When line managers are given responsibility for a process it is particularly important that, as process owners, they pay attention to the views and interests of staff for which they bear no direct line management responsibility.

The ISO/IEC 20000 audit

However process ownership is allocated, an audit will check whether or not the ownership is effective in improving the process and that processes are appropriately integrated. This includes both internal and external support groups, as many processes span the organizational boundaries between external suppliers, the service provider and the customer's business activities.

Example metrics and audit evidence

The metrics and audit evidence shown in Tables 7 and 8 below are only illustrations, as described in *Example metrics and audit evidence* in Chapter 2.

Table 7 – Example metrics linked to management commitment

Metric	Type of metric	Purpose and ISO/IEC 20000 objective
Management commitment	Frequency of management communication sessions of service management and service improvements	Through leadership and actions, top/executive management **shall** provide evidence of its commitment to developing, implementing and improving its service management capability within the context of the organization's business and customers' requirements
Management accountability	Appointment of a single manager with appropriate responsibilities	Management **shall**: d) appoint a member of management responsible for the co-ordination and management of all services

Table 8 – Example audit evidence for requirements

Objective and requirement	Example audit evidence
Objective: To provide a management system, including policies and a framework to enable the effective management and implementation of all IT services.	
Management **shall**:	
a) establish the service management policy, objectives and plans	• Number and status of policies • Status of objectives • Currency and quality of plans
b) communicate the importance of meeting the service management objectives and the need for continual improvement	• Management communications • Management actions supporting the public commitment is real in practice
g) conduct reviews of service management, at planned intervals, to ensure continuing suitability, adequacy and effectiveness	• Review agenda • Review minutes • Review action plans • Audit trail of actions being completed to timetable

CHAPTER 4

The PDCA cycle: An overview

Introduction

ISO/IEC 20000 is a management system standard, i.e. a standard that includes requirements for a system to establish objectives and policies that will support achievement of the objectives. In ISO/IEC 20000 the system is provided by the Plan-Do-Check-Act (PDCA) cycle and other closely related management processes, such as management responsibilities, competence, awareness and training.

This chapter gives a brief overview of the PDCA cycle and an overview of the role of the PDCA cycle in integrated service management. The PDCA cycle also applies to other management processes in ISO/IEC 20000, such as the processes used for the planning and implementing new and changed services, covered by clause 5 of ISO/IEC 20000-1, described in Chapter 9.

The PDCA cycle is particularly important for service management processes as service management should be the subject of frequent review and improvement to keep them optimized. Sometimes improvements deliver a capability that provides the foundation for future service and process improvements.

Each stage in the PDCA cycle is described in Chapters 5 to 8.

The four stages

The four stages of the PDCA cycle are described in a note in ISO/IEC 20000-1, 4 and are defined overleaf.

Definition: Plan, do, check, act

plan

establish the objectives and processes necessary to deliver results in accordance with customer requirements and the organization's policies

do

implement the processes

check

monitor and measure processes and services against policies, objectives and requirements and report the results

act

take actions to continually improve process performance

Inputs and outputs

The PDCA cycle shown in ISO/IEC 20000 is duplicated in Figure 13. The PDCA cycle takes a wide range of inputs, including those directly or indirectly from all service management processes, consequently each of the stages in the PDCA cycle applies to processes in the scope of ISO/IEC 20000.

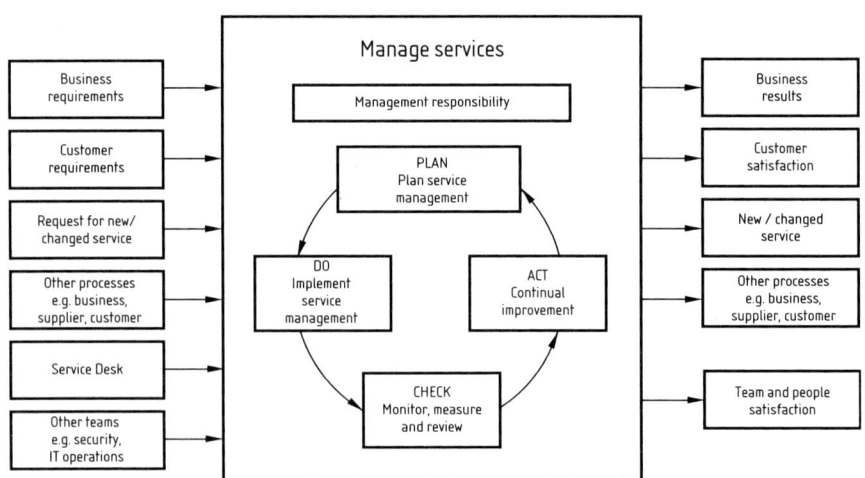

Figure 13 – Plan-Do-Check-Act cycle

ISO/IEC 20000 requires each service management process to provide input to the overall planning and management of services by the PDCA cycle. The PDCA cycle in turn provides input to each service management process. This flow of information is part of the integration of the service management processes, other management processes and the PDCA cycle.

Without effective communication of good information, decisions made within each individual service management process will be uncontrolled and uncoordinated. For example, information on the customer's new business needs must flow from the business relationship management process to the service level management process, so that decisions can be made on a revised SLA. At the same time information must flow to the supplier management process, as a new SLA may not be achievable without a change to the supplier's commitments.

If a change to the supplier's contract is required this is done via the supplier management process and the information is fed back into other processes, including the service level management process.

In addition the service level management process may also need to ensure the service provider's internal agreements that support the SLA are also revised, for the same reason.

Getting the correct balance between the changes to an SLA and any underpinning agreements may take several reiterations. Each time there must be no ambiguity about which process is in control of which part of decision making.

CHAPTER 5

The 'Plan' stage (ISO/IEC 20000-1, 4.1)

Introduction

One of the most common questions on ISO/IEC 20000 is regarding plan or plans (and how they relate).

Planning service management is fundamental to integrating service management processes and achieving ISO/IEC 20000. This chapter describes clause 4.1, *Plan service management (Plan)*.

The planning cycle

The 'Plan' stage of the PDCA cycle initially plans the implementation of service management.

Subsequently, the 'Plan' stage of the cycle plans improvements identified during the 'Check' stage of the cycle, described in Chapter 7.

When service management has not been established at all the initial plan will be complex, require long-term activities and may involve considerable increase in short-term expenditure before savings are provided by increased efficiency.

If service management is in place, but has been badly implemented and uncoordinated, the plans may have to be even more extensive, as bad practices will need to be corrected. There also may be difficulties from the need to adapt, integrate or replace tools used for service management. For example, some common deficiencies in service management integration are rooted in unsuitable automation of processes.

For many service providers the initial planning is less challenging as most service providers aiming to achieve ISO/IEC 20000 do so from a starting point of most service management processes being of a reasonable standard. In this case the initial plan is predominantly that of improving existing processes and filling gaps where processes are missing or incomplete.

Many of those involved in day-to-day delivery of a service will not have been involved in large projects or managed a project themselves. In order to make best use of the operational skills and experience that these staff bring to process and service improvements, it may help for them to have some project or programme management training. Allowing some time for adjustment to new ways of working is also usually advisable.

Contents of the service management plan

The topics required in a plan are described in the sections from *Scope of service management* to *Quality management*.

A service provider may need to add additional topics and some recommendations are included in ISO/IEC 20000-2. These are described in the section *Other topics for the plan.*

Scope of service management

Scope for the service management plan

The scope of service management and of individual processes must be based on things that can be unambiguously:

- sized;
- counted;
- described;
- kept current.

The scope defined in the service management plan will be influenced by whether the service provider is aiming to make phased changes or one large change.

There are many ways of defining the scope of service management. ISO/IEC 20000-2 refers to options for scoping based on:

- location;
- organizational unit;
- service.

Organization and location may be either or both that of the service provider's and that of customer(s). For example, a service provider may initially implement full service management for only their head office services, implementing processes at other locations in later phases, and thereby increasing the scope.

The scope for the service management plan based on location is illustrated in Figure 14. The 'tick' indicates that the location performs processes that meet (or are to be improved to meet) the requirements for the clause in the column heading. This is a high level summary, as each clause contains several requirements and so a further level of detail covering each requirement individually may be necessary for scoping of planned improvements.

Other examples are similar, but with the rows occupied by organizational units, services or other suitable elements of the service provider's scope.

	ISO/IEC 20000-1 clauses	3.1 Management responsibility	3.2 Documentation	3.3 Competence/awareness /training	4.1 PDCA - Plan	4.2 PDCA - Do	4.3 PDCA - Check	6.5 Capacity	6.6 Information security	7.2 Supplier	8.1 Incident	8.2 Problem	9.1 Configuration	9.2 Change	10.1 Release
Service, organization or location	Birmingham	✓	✓	✗	✗	✓	✗	✗	✗	✗	✓	✓	✓	✓	✗
	Delhi	✓	✓	✓	✓	✓	✓	✓	✓	✓	✓	✓	✓	✓	✓
	Milan	✓	✓	✓	✓	✓	✓	✗	✗	✓	✓	✓	✓	✓	✓
	Paris	✓	✓	✓	✓	✓	✓	✓	✓	✓	✓	✓	✓	✓	✓
	Singapore	✓	✓	✓	✓	✓		✓	✓	✓	✓	✗	✗	✗	✗
	Tokyo	✓	✓	✓	✓	✓		✓	✓	✓	✓	✓	✓	✓	✓

Figure 14 – Scope based on location (illustrative)

For a commercial service provider with multiple customers, the scope of service management for the plan may be limited to the service for a single customer, several customers or all customers. Where the scope is limited to only some customers there may be some processes in the scope of the audit that are common to all customers. In this case, the auditor may check all the relevant records, not only those records that apply to the customers within the scope of the audit.

When services are used to define the scope, the services are normally those that are defined in a service catalogue, as described in BIP 0033, *Managing end-to-end services*. If the definitions used in the service catalogue are not suitable for defining the scope of service management it is likely that the service catalogue will also not meet the requirement for a service provider to have a repository of information on the services.

The three parameters, location, organizational unit and service, are examples and can be supplemented or replaced by alternatives, such as assets, infrastructure configuration items or types of technology.

Scope for an audit

A scope statement is also required for an audit, as described in BIP 0030, *Management decisions.* It is only possible to meet the scope requirements for an audit if the service provider can provide evidence for each requirement and that they have control of each process.

Objectives of service management

The combination of policies, objectives and service management plans define management intentions for service management. Policies and objectives serve different purposes.

Policies are a management direction and governance mechanism (i.e. controls). Policies are the overall general intentions and may have no time limit. They normally represent process and service qualities and are described in Chapter 3.

Objectives are a mechanism for setting goals or required results (referred to as outcomes by clause 4.4 of ISO/IEC 20000). Objectives give details of specific achievements and usually include specifics such as dates for the results to be achieved.

The mix of policies and objectives is useful in that the policies set the general direction and the objectives the specific goals and results to be achieved.

Example objectives include:

- increase customer satisfaction by 10%;
- reduce low priority support calls by 5% per year by increasing the level of end user training;
- reduce dependency on key individuals over the next two years with the introduction of individual knowledge transfer plans;
- improve server capacity by 30% over the next six months with a review of email usage.

For some service providers, there are many forms of legal and regulatory requirements. It is advisable for these requirements to be reflected in the objectives and policies for service management, e.g. Sarbanes Oxley, the Basel 2 Accord, Health and Safety, and Security. Otherwise the service provider may discover too late that they cannot meet legal or regulatory requirements.

Process control

Not all processes will be implemented, changed or improved at the same time and the service management plan may include several phases for the introduction of processes or improvements to those already in place.

The integrated nature of service management processes (and of the PDCA cycle and other processes) means that as one process is changed another is very likely to be affected. This dependency needs to be clear in the service management plan.

Using industry standard names and terms for processes in the plan can be much simpler for a service provider. For example, it makes training easier, particularly for new staff who may already have been trained in best practice service management. If the service provider uses alternative process names to those used in ISO/IEC 20000 the mapping of local names to those in ISO/IEC 20000 is helpful for the plan and to the auditor, either being part of it or cross-referenced within the plan.

Management framework

ISO/IEC 20000 requires the management framework, as a minimum, to describe:

- management roles and responsibilities;
- management of suppliers.

Clarity on the roles and responsibilities of those involved in supplier management are particularly important to the management framework as services are normally the end result of a complex supply chain. This may involve several suppliers, a service provider and potentially many different groups of users. Complex supply chains may enable the service provider to deliver the most cost-effective service by using 'best of breed' suppliers, cover remote locations or to provide additional resources at short notice, or to meet a short-term need.

If the business relationship management process owner does not have direct responsibility for customer satisfaction, the person who does will normally be included in the plan. This is particularly important if the plan will be introducing changes that will be visible to the customers. Roles and responsibility mapping are described in BIP 0031, *Why people matter.*

Issue and risk management

This requirement includes risks such as:

- conflicting changes;
- high-risk changes;
- unrealistic changes;

- unsuitable resources (people and technical);
- major incidents or disasters diverting resources.

Best practice project or programme management and the change and configuration management processes cover this requirement.

Example: Escalation of risks

Service desk managers handle internal risks, such as issues relating to service desk services, including telephony, attrition, communications etc.

However, the senior responsible owner may need to handle risks/issues affecting services such as peaks/troughs in volumes of calls presented to the service desk at certain periods.

These need to be discussed with the customer and it may not be appropriate for the service desk manager to do this if it is an issue relating to other processes, such as the business or service level management processes or the capacity management processes.

Key point:

Risks and issues can be managed locally and then escalated to the next level, e.g. process owner, senior responsible owner.

Interfacing to projects

Those projects of interest to service management planning are those that are creating or modifying services. The range of projects is potentially very wide, e.g. a new service or a facilities management project affecting power supplies. This is linked to the requirements in clause 5 of ISO/IEC 20000-1, and includes a requirement for the introduction of new or changed services, described in Chapter 9.

Resources, facilities and budgets

As for most projects, particularly large or complex ones, the resources, facilities and budgets required will be clearly defined in the plan, as is required by all best practice project or programme management methods. Key aspects of resources, facilities and budgets are listed below.

Resources:

- people;
- technology;
- applications;

- databases
- data/information
- suppliers.

Facilities:

- space/accommodation;
- secure storage;
- technology;
- security.

Budget:

- cost-benefit case;
- source of funds;
- timing of fund release/cash flow for each stage;
- capital and depreciation implications;
- revenue;
- financial authorization for costs being incurred;
- management of budget variances.

Tools

Although the use of tools for the support and automation of processes is not included in the requirements, where tools are in place they must be included in the plan. This is because there is a relationship between process, procedure and the availability of suitable tools.

Processes must be simple if automation is not possible. Where tools are available, processes may be designed to achieve much more and to do so at lower cost and with higher reliability. For example, service reporting, which is essential to the integration of processes, can become expensive, slow and error prone if the process is largely manual, as data produced by one process is manually transferred to another. If tools are not available, processes must be as simple as possible.

Any change to processes may impact the tools used. The reverse is also the case. Where the processes are not well-defined, a change to the tool used by one process may impact the ability of another process to function. For example, the data collected by incident management may not meet the requirements of problem management or the data stored by configuration management may not be usable by continuity management.

Integrated service management manages this risk and delivers greater efficiency as a consequence.

Quality management

Quality criteria, including current service levels, service targets and goals for improvements need to be agreed and included in the plan. Other information such as the timetable for reviews, internal and external or certification audits, is useful. Information on plans to achieve other standards (such as ISO/IEC 90003, *Guidelines for the application of ISO 9001:2000 to computer software*) may impact service management and should be included or cross-referenced.

This information is part of best practice project management and planning. It is advisable for the service provider aiming to achieve ISO/IEC 20000 to adopt a formal project or programme management methodology. ISO/IEC 20000 does not specify which methodology should be used and the quality of the methodology will not normally be included in the audit. However, if an inadequate or inappropriate methodology is adopted, or a good one is used badly, the service management plan will not meet the requirements.

Other topics for the plan

It is also recommended that the service management plan should cater for service management process and service changes.

Depending on an individual service provider's circumstances, other topics may be required for the plan. These include:

- the approach to changing the plan and the service defined by the plan;
- how the organization will demonstrate continuing quality control, e.g. interim audits, a schedule of major reviews of performances and results;
- implementation of a performance evaluation framework, e.g. balanced scorecard.

Structure and management of the plans

The following are some of the most common questions on ISO/IEC 20000.

- Is it one plan or lots of plans?
- How do all the plans fit together?
- Should we use a programme management approach or several projects?

How a service provider arranges its plans and planning depends on the individual circumstances.

When establishing service management, an overall service management plan is appropriate. The overall service management plan is a living document, subject to change as circumstances change and improvements are implemented.

A service management plan typically includes or references:

- policies (which are more effective if brief and to the point);
- the service provider's objectives in implementing service management;
- the mapping of manager and roles, such as process owner;
- the structure of the service management plans including any improvement plans.

Typically, the person who decides on the approach for the plan or programme will be the 'Senior responsible owner', as described in Chapter 3.

Whatever method is used it will be necessary during an audit to demonstrate how each planning requirement is managed by linking it to the corresponding roles, responsibilities and processes and services. The plan itself should include details of 'who does what'. This is normal project or programme management best practice and not unique to service management and the PDCA cycle.

The service management plan may be one plan or many plans. If there is more that one plan at the top level there should be clearly-defined delegation of the subordinate plans. However control is achieved for each plan and the overall plan, no plans should be separate from any other plans or there will be a risk of overlaps and gaps that may cause issues and risks in implementing service management.

With a programme management approach activities are coordinated and are all driven by the same set of service management policies and objectives. With best practice programme management the benefits from the whole programme are greater than the sum of the individual work streams. This is because the deliverables of each work stream are also integrated.

Work streams could be a mix of the establishment of new processes, improvements in existing processes, cascading of changes to policies or objectives down through the policy, process, procedure hierarchy and development and implementation of a staff training plan.

For a set of changes where one process being changed can ripple through and impact others, a programme approach avoids the risk of a silo approach, where each process is handled as if it operated in complete isolation.

Figure 15 (on the next page) shows the combination of a programme of service improvements combined with a management of change programme.

A programme management approach also works well with management of change initiatives. The results of the programme are the ability and willingness to change, as well as knowing what needs to change and how it should change. This approach avoids the risk of ignoring how the service provider's staff, suppliers, customers and users of the service feel about the change.

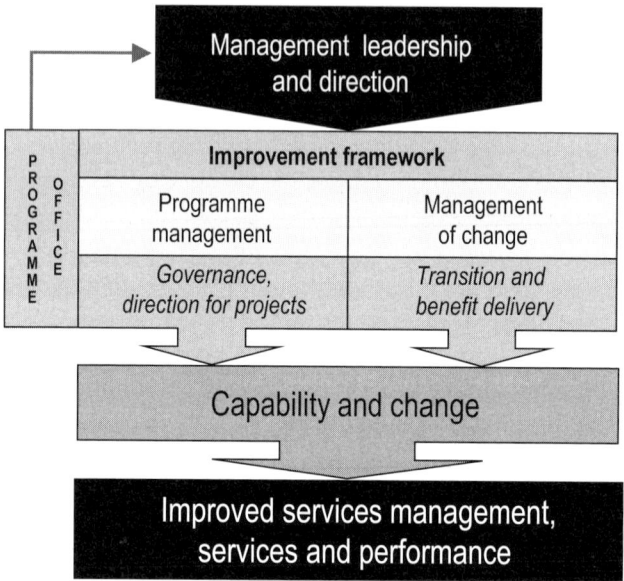

Figure 15 – Programme management and management of change

A programme approach is more likely to be appropriate if there are many different areas where changes are required, e.g. where service management is being established for the first time and most topics in the scope of ISO/IEC 20000 need some attention. If the service provider has well-established processes and meets the requirements a single project approach may be adequate to keep the processes optimized.

It is important that the selected approach ensures that the underlying service management processes are consistent with each other. For example, if the planning introduces changes to a process it must not duplicate or conflict with other processes.

For example, a change to logging practices (such as the definition of incidents, problems, service requests, changes or queries) should not disrupt the service reporting, problem management and change management processes.

Organizations may have several plans if each aspect of the implementation or improvements is managed by different managers.

An example of how plans may be structured is shown in Figure 16. In this example the service management plan is composed of many subordinate plans.

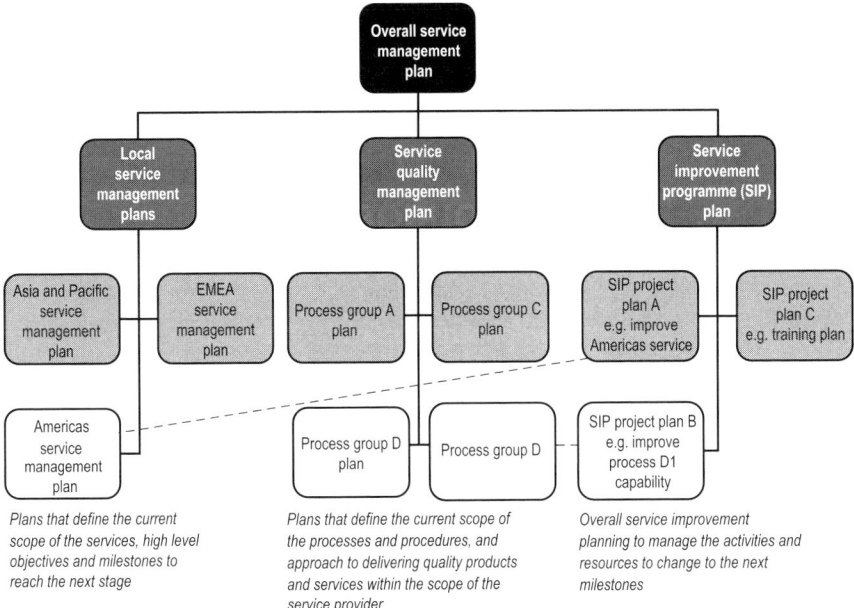

Figure 16 – Example structure of service management plans

The example in Figure 16 could apply to a large service provider operating in many countries and providing many services. In this example, responsibilities for subordinate plans are allocated to many different managers, each with a specific scope and role.

Process specific plans

Where the service provider also relies on some local, process specific plans, it requires that process specific plans be compatible with the overall service management plan. This is similar to grouping of plans under an overall plan, as shown in Figure 16.

There must be no conflicts over the results of local plans, other process specific plans or the activities of the PDCA cycle. Process changes, however they are planned for must not have a detrimental impact on other processes and there must also be a link for information flow between local, process specific plans and the PDCA cycle.

Many service providers manage their process specific plans under the umbrella of service improvement programme management.

The requirement for process-specific plans to be compatible with the overall service management plan means that when improvements are identified and implemented locally by one of the service management processes, the information on this must be fed into the overall service management plan for use by the PDCA cycle.

Phased process implementation

Aiming for integrated processes does not mean that all processes must be implemented in a 'big bang' approach.

Phased implementation is lower risk and has financial advantages. For example, processes may be implemented in the order that will bring the greatest benefits first for that particular service provider, so that the improvements help fund the cost of later phases, or at least make the cost more easily justified and more acceptable.

A good plan for phased implementation has a very clear view of what is to be achieved in the long term. ISO/IEC 20000 provides a framework for the overall plan, and each requirement can be a milestone for the plan, with 'Achieving ISO/IEC 20000' as the ultimate goal.

Where there has been a holistic view of service management and a top-down approach during the earliest planning stage, planning will be based on an understanding of how information and control should flow between individual processes and will be much better as a consequence. Processes can then be implemented in phases, with each phase based on an understanding of the interfaces that will exist when all processes have been implemented. The processes will deliver much greater benefits as a consequence.

 Example: Service management improvements and SLAs

SLAs (service level agreements) are important in service level management and are required by ISO/IEC 20000. As a result, a service provider may present detailed SLAs for authorization at the very start of an improvement programme. However tempting this may be, this approach can be counter-productive when other service management processes are largely missing, immature or inadequate. Customers may refuse to sign the SLA and continue to resist this even when the service management and service have noticeably improved.

To develop SLAs that add value, a service provider must have a detailed understanding of the customer's business, a good working relationship with the customer (requiring effective business relationship management) and access to historic information on service levels and workloads in terms that reflect the customer's view of the service (from an effective service reporting process and other service management processes).

Key point:

Correct timing is important and can make or break the success of a service and service management improvement programme.

Handling changes to the plan

The plans themselves are under the control of the change management process and therefore also included in configuration management. At each stage roles and responsibilities must be clear for:

- review;
- authorization;
- communicating the details;
- implementation (the 'Do' stage of the PDCA cycle);
- maintenance.

Testing the plans

For those with experience in project or programme management, it may be common sense that plans must be tested. It is advisable to check the assumptions that form the basis of plans, e.g. that people will be available when required, that there will be no major conflicting demands, that the budget will be available as required etc.

Details such as the practicality of deliverables being produced on time, the realism (or otherwise) of the estimates for the work required for each activity and stage, even the overall deliverables are all areas of a plan that need to be tested.

One method is to pilot changes where and when possible, so that experience can be gained and fed into the next stage of planning as 'lessons learned'.

Acceptance testing should also be carried out.

Example metrics and audit evidence

Illustrations of metrics and audit evidence only are included in Tables 9 and 10 as a definitive list is not possible, as described in the section *Example metrics and audit evidence* in Chapter 2.

Table 9 – Example metrics for service management planning

Metric	Type of metric	Purpose and ISO/IEC 20000 objective
Efficiency	Reduced level of resources and time required as ratio of number of changes	Deliver results according to objectives in the service management plan
Successful change	Sign off by the business and customer that the service and service levels are aligned with the business objectives	The service is deliverable and manageable at the agreed service quality
Cost	Percentage variance from estimated costs	The service is deliverable and manageable at the agreed cost
Efficiency	Service delivered within estimated time, resource and costs	The service is deliverable and manageable at the agreed cost

Table 10 – Example audit evidence for requirements

Objective and requirement	Example audit evidence
Objective: To plan the implementation and delivery of service management.	
Service management **shall** be planned	• Service management plan or plans • Rationale for structure and relationship of different parts of the overall plan
The plans **shall** at a minimum define	
a) the scope of the service provider's service management	Scope document, including changes to scope of service management with any planned phased improvements
e) the interfaces between service management processes and the manner in which the activities are to be co-ordinated	• Documents describing the interfaces • Process & procedure for control of plans when there are multiple plans, including control of local/process based plans

CHAPTER 6

The 'Do' stage (ISO/IEC 20000-1, 4.2)

Introduction

The ultimate proof of the effectiveness of any plan is that the implementation of the plan is successful and provides the results and benefits that were intended and expected.

The plan produced for establishing service management processes, and subsequent improvements described in Chapter 5, is implemented in the 'Do' stage of the PDCA cycle. This chapter describes the requirements and recommendations for this stage.

Allocating funding

Many organizations have a history of short-term enthusiasm for new ideas and new technology. Many have a track record of starting initiatives such as the implementation of best practice service management and failing to complete even the first phase, only to restart a few years later. This is usually due to inadequate management commitment or unrealistic expectations on what can be achieved.

A test of management commitment to best practice service management includes the funds and budgets committed during the planning stage actually being released for use during implementation (and subsequent delivery). Lack of commitment by management is shown if funds are directed to another initiative without there being a sound reason. There are occasions when short-notice changes to funds are unavoidable, e.g. the organization is required to cut all budgets because the financial state of the organization is precarious, or because another initiative has priority because it is required for regulatory or legislative requirements.

If funds are reduced the plans should be reconsidered as it is normally more effective to implement improvements more slowly than to attempt major changes with an inadequate budget.

Who does what?

A theme of ISO/IEC 20000 is that it is essential for there to be no ambiguity about who does what and when. This avoids confusion that creates errors, reduces efficiency and can create a stressful working environment for the customer, user and both the service provider's staff and management. Any plan that has not made this clear must be corrected before implementation.

It may be necessary to involve new people if the time taken to get agreement to the plan and funding is extended, as those people originally expected to take particular roles may no longer be available. This is good practice project and programme management and not unique to the PDCA cycle.

Documentation

As described in BIP 0030, *Management decisions and documentation*, documents and records are an important part of service management, although quality and usefulness does not normally increase with length and complexity of the prose. The 'Do' stage of the PDCA cycle requires documents to be used, to be useful and to be kept up to date. Those specifically mentioned include:

- the plans themselves;
- policies;
- definitions for each process or set of processes;
- procedures.

Risks

Risks identified during the planning stage need to be reassessed just before implementation and monitored during the rest of the 'Do' stage.

Complacency arising from the view that rigorous risk assessment and management during the 'Plan' stage is sufficient should be avoided as new risks will arise over time. For example the customer may plan to implement changes to business activities at a time when the service management plan is at a critical stage, causing a potential clash in priorities. Mergers, acquisitions and legal changes are all examples.

Other risks include the dependency on particular individuals, e.g. key individuals move into new roles, without a fully trained and experienced replacement being available.

Human resources

One of the risks described in the previous section was the over-reliance on key individuals. Other risks include:

- avoiding or managing resistance to change;
- ensuring management understand and are committed to the plan;
- motivating staff affected directly and indirectly;
- developing existing staff skills;
- recruiting any necessary new staff;
- managing staff continuity as roles change or are established.

It is important that the plan and how it is implemented takes into account the time and effort required to consolidate new working practices. Policies, processes and procedures are not simply established by publication of a relevant set of documents, however well written they may be. Change to existing work practices requires:

- communications;
- re-education;
- understanding of the objectives in making the changes;
- how and for what the person will be rewarded for success;
- additional support or mentoring for a period of time;
- and if necessary re-education and retraining after the initial implementation.

It is necessary to train staff in both service management and technical topics. Other information is provided in BIP 0031, *Why people matter*.

ISO/IEC 20000-2 also notes that a person who is ideal for planning and implementing service management and other service improvements may not be appropriate for longer-term improvements or day-to-day delivery of a service and vice versa. Allocating of roles and responsibilities, recruiting new staff etc., should not neglect this. A person allocated a role must have the right type of personality and demonstrate the correct behaviours as well as appropriate skills for that role.

Continuing resource management

Managing the teams who provide the service requires:

- facilities;
- budget;
- resources, e.g. automation;
- managing people.

The auditor will seek evidence that these meet the requirements of the 'Do' stage.

There will often be standard processes driven by organization-wide financial management policies (or standards), which in turn are usually driven by legal or regulatory requirements. As described in BIP 34, *Finance for service managers*, these do not have to be specific to service management.

Progress

This is normal good practice project or programme management. This covers tracking and reporting progress against the plans but with focus on the quality of the service management policies, processes and procedures. An example of a report used for reporting progress against a plan for process improvements is given in Figure 17. This is an example of what is commonly referred to as a 'red, amber, green' (RAG) report or 'Traffic light report', in that it uses red to identify a serious concern, amber for a minor concern that is probably redeemable, and green for a status that is on-time, within budget and where there are no concerns.

Coordination

The planning stage of the PDCA cycle defines the scope of each process, for use as the basis for coordination and integration of the processes. This good practice needs to be protected during process and process improvement implementation and actual delivery. Localized initiatives, even if done with the best of intentions, may damage the existing integration of processes. Preventing this is partly an issue of educating managers and staff in the dangers of isolated and uncoordinated activities. A team of effective process owners who are committed to their responsibilities and work well together can be key to coordination remaining at a high standard.

Delivering the service

The PDCA cycle includes the continued oversight of service management process quality and therefore of service quality and efficiency. This requires a continuing level of rigour, enthusiasm and commitment, which may represent more of a challenge than the original burst of activity when processes are first implemented. Good managers will also identify new opportunities for improvement whilst delivering the service.

Work stream	ISO/IEC 20000-1 clause	Project	Process owner	RAG	Percentage complete	Start	End	Reasons for shortfall / over achievement
W1	3.2	Document library	Ian Jones		36%	29/09/2004	21/06/2005	Technical failures during early stage of project now resolve and most time has been recovered
W2	9.1	Configuration management: Financial asset tracking automated	Karen Brown		56%	01/03/2005	20/03/2006	The information gathered is being collated
W3	6.1	Service level management: new format SLAs and new service catalogue	Janie Patel		70%	01/03/2005	20/03/2006	Awaiting feedback from the customer on actual documents - drafts were agreed during first stage of discussions
W4	3.3	Staff communications / cascade process established	John Smith		15%	12/05/2005	15/02/2006	Pilot milestone delayed by 6 week
W5	10.1	Release management: Improvement of automatic roll-out procedures	Keith O'Connor		64%	13/06/2005	28/01/2006	User forum discussions very supportive, except for agreement on timings and ability to refuse an update
W6	8	Incident and problem management: Implementation of new logging system	Mark Smith		0%	09/01/2006	31/05/2006	Not yet started

Figure 17 – Improvement plan progress report

Example metrics and audit evidence

The examples shown in Tables 11 and 12 are only illustrations as each service provider may meet the requirements by using different metrics.

Table 11 – Example metrics for the 'Do' stage of PDCA

Metric	Type of metric	Purpose and ISO/IEC 20000 objective
Effectiveness	Reduce time to resolve incidents and problems	Deliver results according to objectives in the service management plan
Compliance	Decrease in percentage non-compliances, e.g. software licences	Deliver results in accordance with the organization's policies
Successful change	Service meets service level agreements	The service is deliverable and manageable at the right service quality

Table 12 – Example audit evidence for requirements

Objective and requirement	Example audit evidence
Objective: To implement the service management objectives and plan.	
The service provider **shall** implement the service management plan to manage and deliver the services, including: a) allocation of funds and budgets	Budgets and accounts shown funds are available in practice, and meet the agreed commitments in the plan
b) allocation of roles and responsibilities	Responsibility matrices Action plans allocating activities to those identified as responsible for each role Evidence of successful tracking of activities allocated
h) reporting progress against the plans	Process report, including where slippage has occurred Evidence of how that slippage is assessed and how the risks to the plan from are mitigated

CHAPTER 7

The 'Check' stage
(ISO/IEC 20000-1, 4.3)

Introduction

The driver behind ISO/IEC 20000 and service management improvements is to improve the quality and cost-effectiveness of the service and the customer's satisfaction with it.

Service management established to meet the needs of customers and of the service provider under one set of circumstances may not be appropriate as circumstances change e.g. following a change in the customer's business activities, a merger or even a change in legislation or regulatory requirements.

The objective of the 'Check' stage is to monitor, measure and review that the service management objectives and plan are being achieved. This chapter describes the requirements and recommendations for this stage.

Monitoring and analysis

It is important at any stage of the PDCA cycle, but particularly in the 'Check' stage, to keep in mind that although ISO/IEC 20000 is a process-based standard, it is necessary to monitor services. This is also a benefit to the PDCA cycle in that a deficiency in the service is often due to a deficiency in a process. Identifying the cause may lead to identification of a process improvement, so that correcting one corrects the other.

Figure 18 illustrates a summary report (based on red, amber, green) that can be used to alert the senior responsible owner, or process owners, of the need to check processes. For example, the worsening of the status on major incidents should result in checks on why this has happened – were the major incidents due to failed changes? (In which case either the change management process may need to be improved, or the information from the configuration management process is defective.)

		March	April	May
Major incidents	▽	0	3	6
Incident and problem management	7	1409	1137	1173
Number of calls (operations)	△	2,798	2,617	2,296
Firewall availability	9	100.00%	100.00%	100.00%
Number of std queue (requests in target)	2	47/47	29/30	21/21
Percentage reported and successful service back up	7	99.85%	100.00%	99.00%
Customer satisfaction	7	72.00%	69.00%	71.00%
Percentage of ops performance measures failed	7	13.64%	15.15%	16.66%
Number of operational changes per month	7	202	185	139

KEY

	Action needed	▽	Status has worsened since last month
	Watching brief	△	Status has improved since last month
	No major issues	2	Number of months at same status

Figure 18 – Metrics and the 'Check' stage

In the 'Check' stage it is important to learn from experience. This involves analysis of trends and of individual significant events. This stage of the PDCA cycle is similar to the proactive aspects of service management, such as the problem management process.

The service reporting process, which spans all aspects of service management, is important to this requirement, as described in BIP 0032, *Making metrics work.* Metrics are also important to individual processes and process integration, as it is the flow of useful, timely and accurate information between processes that is the basis of process integration.

All monitoring, measuring and reviewing is required to be done using methods that check whether the processes have achieved planned results. These planned results should have been developed and agreed as part of the original plan, but may have been updated several times if the PDCA cycle has been established for some time.

What constitutes 'planned results' may vary widely. For example, improvement in the cost-effectiveness of a process such as incident management, i.e. a reduction of 30% in the unit cost of resolution of an incident. Another example would be an increase of 20% in customer satisfaction. This is measured by the business relationship management process, but is contributed to by many other processes.

This approach of checking as part of PDCA against planned results is similar to service management practices, where many activities are focused by targets against which 'actuals' are compared.

Topics for monitoring

Topics for monitoring, measurement and analysis are described below. Recommendations include monitoring of services and systems as well as processes. A service provider may choose to include others. As a recommendation, these topics are not compulsory topics for the service provider to monitor. However, the topics represent a tried and tested group that will help the service provider achieve ISO/IEC 20000.

Achievement against defined service targets

It is important that the relationship between the process, process quality and the services that are supported by each process is understood. This understanding should be used in identifying the benefits of improving a service management process on the quality of service delivered and the ability to handle the volume of current and expected activity. For example, improving the incident management process may be linked to a target for reducing the resolution time by 30 minutes for the highest priority incidents and problems.

Service targets are particularly important in service level agreements, internal support agreements, and service commitments in supplier contracts, which are managed via the supplier management process.

By tracking actual service levels against targets the service provider is able to get an objective early warning of any process defects, including defects in the PDCA cycle.

Customer satisfaction

The monitoring of customer satisfaction is within the scope of the business relationship management process, and is included as a requirement by ISO/IEC 20000-1, 7.2.

It is important to the PDCA cycle as it represents the ultimate test of how successful the service provider is in understanding the customer's business needs, how that converts to new services, how it is affected by new or changed service management processes, and finally, how successfully the PDCA has met the business needs of the customer.

Resource utilization

Any good plan or programme includes tracking of resources against the expected level. If this is not done there can be serious problems later in the project as resources are no longer available when they are critical to the plan. Many resources fall into this category, including staff numbers and skills.

Trends

Trends are an important as they allow predictions of what is likely to happen or be achieved in the future. If the prediction is not acceptable the warning provided by the trends gives time for corrective action.

Major non-conformities

It is advisable to have agreed in advance what will be done, who will do it, and, if possible, when they will do it if there is a serious problem with the plan, identified during the check stage. It is also advisable to agree in advance what constitutes a major non-conformance.

Results of reviews

Reviews are also suitable for monitoring what is happening during the 'Check' stage, and can provide a safety net by acting as a catch-all for any topic not monitored. They also provide a vehicle for deciding what should be done if the unexpected happens, and for confirming all is running to plan if no unexpected events or results are observed.

The necessity for management to be involved reflects the scale of this requirement, which encompasses the whole of service management and not just a single process that may or may not be considered defective.

Reviewing progress with improvements

Figure 19 illustrates an example of a report that would be used to check progress with planned improvements. It is similar in intent, but has a different style to reports such as those illustrated by Figure 17 in Chapter 6 and Figure 18 in Chapter 7.

Weekly status

Document / Process	Status	Draft Due	Issued	Last Review	Next Review	200Y				
						Aug	Sep	Oct	Nov	Dec
SIP Reporting V2.0.doc	Issued	09-Jul-0Y	08-Aug-0Y	13-Nov-0Y	12-Feb-04	x			x	
SIP Reporting Example Weekly Report.xls	Issued	09-Jul-0Y	08-Aug-0Y	13-Nov-0Y	12-Feb-04	x			x	x
SIP QP & Gov V2.0.doc	Issued	21-Jul-0Y	08-Aug-0Y	13-Nov-0Y	12-Feb-04	x			x	
SIP IM Process V1.1.doc	Issued	01-Aug-0Y	09-Oct-0Y		08-Dec-0Y					x
SIP PM Process V1.1.doc	Issued	07-Aug-0Y	09-Oct-0Y		08-Dec-0Y					x
SIP Apps Packs Template V1.0.doc	Issued	22-Sep-0Y	22-Sep-0Y		19-Dec-0Y					x
SIP TP SLM Template V0.2	Reviewed	10-Nov-0Y								
SIP Decommissioning	Reviewed	24-Nov-0Y			24-Feb-04				x	
SIP Induction Pack	Not Start									
Audits		**Due Date**								
A-PDCA 01 Review		12-Aug-0Y		12-Aug-0Y	26-Nov-0Y	x			x	
A-PDCA 02 Review		15-Aug-0Y				x				
ISO/IEC 20000 Inspections		23-Sep-0Y					x			

Figure 19 – Example report for reviewing progress with improvements

Audits

The importance of objectivity

Senior management involved in a review may well also be closely involved in the processes that are being reviewed. Under these circumstances, it is difficult for senior management to remain objective. As a consequence it is required that an audit programme should be included in the 'Check' stage of the PDCA cycle. This is separate from any independent certification audit that is required to achieve ISO/IEC 20000. The type of audit referred to in ISO/IEC 20000-1 and which is described here is an audit done as a check on the status of the plans developed in the first 'Plan' stage of the PDCA cycle.

The type of audit referred to in ISO/IEC 20000 normally involves an independent auditor. This auditor may be an internal or external person, but it is important that the auditor is not a senior responsible owner, a process owner or involved in closely related day-to-day operational activities. This is necessary to ensure the audit programme is carried out objectively and independently.

Many of the benefits of an audit are due to the objectivity of the person or people doing the audit. Objectivity means it is easier to take a balanced view as an impartial auditor will be independent of the team that have championed the benefits of service management, of the management commitment required, of the PDCA cycle and of meeting the requirements.

However tempting it is to use someone who has been involved because they understand how it all works and can do the audit faster (and cheaper) an auditor who is not impartial cannot be as effective and the results will not have the same credibility. For this reason, ISO/IEC 20000-1 expressly forbids anyone auditing work with which they have been personally involved. This excludes not just the person who manages the plan, but also anyone who was involved in a more junior capacity.

Audits may be done by:

- an internal audit group;
- staff from another part of IT;
- external consultants.

Audit criteria

It is important to be clear, in advance of the audit, what the audit is to achieve and what scope it is to have, i.e. what changes or improvements are to be checked. ISO/IEC 20000 obviously provides assistance on this aspect of audits.

The audit is required to take into account the relative importance and status of the processes and of each area to be audited, as well as the results of any previous audits.

This allows the audit to be more effective, in that it can target the most important aspects of the service and of the service management processes. The audit will also be able to probe any areas of weakness that should have been corrected since the last audit.

To avoid compromising on the quality of the audit, there is a requirement that the criteria, scope, frequency and methods are defined in advance. This generally increases the overall benefits from doing an audit, as there is no uncertainty about why it is being done.

Audit scope

The scope of the audit required as part of the 'Check' stage should be determined by the scope of the plans developed in the 'Plan' stage of the PDCA cycle. If the plan (or plans) addresses only a small number of topics that need fine-tuning, the scope may be very limited and specific to these topics. Conversely, if service management has only just been established, or has been in place for a long time but has degraded through neglect, the scope may have to be limited so that the results of the 'Check' stage can be fed back for the identification of quick fixes and rapid action in the 'Act' stage, or to be considered when the plan is under review. For example, it should be decided whether the audit is to examine all:

- processes;
- locations;
- services;
- customers.

Frequency

There is no single frequency that is appropriate for all service providers and all PDCA cycles. If the service and service management processes are being changed rapidly, frequent audits are likely to be most effective. For example, a major audit annually, with quarterly or six-monthly interim audits (examining less detail or only key issues) may well be suitable. For more slowly changing service providers, an annual audit may well be more than adequate.

When deciding the frequency of internal audits and checks, the degree of risk involved in a process, its frequency of operation and its past history of problems should be among the factors that are taken into account.

It is also recommended that in common with external certification and re-certification audits, internal audits and checks should be planned, carried out competently and recorded, as they would be for an independent external audit. This will encourage a level of rigour that is advantageous to the PDCA cycle.

Whatever frequency is agreed, the service provider and in particular the 'senior responsible owner' should resist the temptation to delay the agreed audit until 'things are a little less busy'. This delay generally becomes permanent and the audit is never done.

Methods

The method by which an auditor is to make a judgment must be clear. A certification audit has to be against ISO/IEC 20000-1, as this contains requirements. Other types of external audits or internal audits do not lead to certification, but can be against one or more of:

- service management plan;
- ISO/IEC 20000-1;
- ISO/IEC 20000-1 and ISO/IEC 20000-2 together;
- suitable checklists, such as BIP 0015, *IT Service Management – Self assessment workbook'*.

Implementing best practice service management and achieving ISO/IEC 20000 requires a more sophisticated approach than simply providing evidence against each of the '**shalls**' in isolation. The relationship between the processes and between the requirements is an important aspect of integrated service management and of the overall requirements of ISO/IEC 20000.

The whys and whats

ISO/IEC 20000-1 includes a requirement that the objective of service management reviews, assessments and audits shall be recorded together with the findings of such audits and reviews and any remedial actions identified. Checklist 3 summarizes the key points.

The service provider is also required to understand and communicate any significant areas of non-compliance or concerns. It also requires the service provider to ensure that this information is made available to those who are affected or are responsible for this.

Checklist 3: Objective of the reviews, assessments and audits
What was done?
How was it done?
Who did it?
Who was it done for?
What were the results?
Who needs to be told of the results?
Were the objectives achieved?
What should happen next?

Checking the existing scope of processes

Where service management is already in place, the scope of each process also needs to be reviewed to identify existing overlaps, confusion or any gaps in processes. The results are input to a plan for improvements.

The improvements may involve changes to roles and responsibilities and possibly to the service provider's organizational structure.

Improvements

The results of reviews, assessments and audits is input to a plan for improving the service, either as part of the overarching PDCA cycle or localized to a single process, under the control of the relevant process owner. Even if the improvement activity is localized, the activity should not be isolated or parochial in its effect, i.e. the improvement is still coordinated within the PDCA cycle and should be compatible with any other planned Improvements and changes.

Correcting established service management

Many organizations implement their service management processes 'bottom-up', with individual processes implemented by individual best practice enthusiasts, working on an *ad hoc* basis and possibly with a parochial viewpoint. With a 'bottom-up' approach, problems arise from variants in processes that should be standardized if overall efficiency is to be improved. Other problems arise because processes developed in isolation are unlikely to be properly integrated.

The 'bottom-up' approach mainly occurs when senior management do not yet understand or support service management as a whole.

The processes developed in isolation normally then have to be to be integrated retrospectively. The following serve as examples.

When service management processes are in place, but not integrated effectively, it is usually necessary to carry out a major service improvement programme with a top-down approach. This may need to introduce management commitment and policies for the first time. It is also often necessary to ensure that processes are linked to and underpin the policies and that procedures are linked to and underpin the processes. Service reporting will normally need to be reviewed, streamlined and substantially improved as integration is reliant on information passing between processes.

Example metrics and audit evidence

The example metrics and audit evidence given in Tables 13 and 14 are only illustrations, as described in *Example metrics and audit evidence* in Chapter 2.

Table 13 – Example metrics for the 'Check' stage of PDCA

Metric	Type of metric	Purpose and ISO/IEC 20000 objective
Reduced exposure to risk	Reduced number of errors introduced to the live services from changes	Deliver results according to objectives in the service management plan
Reduced exposure to risk	Reduced number of major incidents and outages (un- availability) caused by poorly managed change	Deliver results according to objectives in the service management plan
Operational risk	Number of errors introduced to the live services from the new or changed service	The service is deliverable and manageable at the right cost and service quality
Successful service delivery	Customer satisfaction with the service	The service is deliverable and manageable at the right service quality

Table 14 – Example audit evidence for requirements

Objective and requirement	Example audit evidence
Objective: To monitor, measure and review that the service management objectives and plan are being achieved.	
These methods **shall** demonstrate the ability of the processes to achieve planned results	Comparison of the relevant policies, service management objectives with the timetable of events and the process results Example process results include: Reduced time to fix All of service level agreements valid Reports on customer satisfaction Gap analysis of the expected results of PDCA and the actual results
The audit criteria, scope, frequency and methods **shall** be defined	Agreed audit criteria compared to actual audit performed Auditor criteria compared to actual auditor selected Audit timetable
Any significant areas of non-compliance or concern **shall** be communicated to relevant parties	Gap analysis Escalation of serious issues Communications to process owners, senior responsible owner, line managers and customers

CHAPTER **8**

The 'Act' stage (ISO/IEC 20000-1, 4.4)

Introduction

The implementation of the overall service management plan is dependent on the effectiveness of each of the four stages of the PDCA cycle. This includes the 'Act' stage, which has the objective:

> *'To improve the effectiveness and efficiency of service delivery and management.'*

Service improvements

Service providers who have achieved ISO/IEC 20000 have done so partly because they have recognized that there is always the potential to make the delivery of services more effective and efficient. A service provider of this type continues to seek ways of improving their service management processes in order to improve their service.

ISO/IEC 20000 is mainly targeted on process improvements; however, other improvements include any or all of people, technology or systems. For example, the staff may be developed to have a much higher standard of service management understanding, become more targeted on what matters or work more effectively from improved management (and management may develop improved leadership skills).

Similarly, it may be recognized that a process is best practice but manually intensive and error prone, so that automation will give a significant improvement to the reliability of the process as well as the speed with which the process life cycle is completed.

The cyclic nature of PDCA means that as soon as the 'Act' stage is complete, the cycle restarts with review and revisions of the service management plans by the 'Plan' stage.

Which improvements?

It is advisable for a service provider to be aware that potential improvements made come from many sources. For example:

- the customer and business plans;
- customer satisfaction surveys;
- sector knowledge of better ways of providing a service;
- process owners;
- support staff;
- process information, including service reports;
- automation opportunities;
- security alerts;
- internal audits;
- complaints.

It is recommended by ISO/IEC 20000-2 that a service provider should encourage suggestions for improvements. This is described in BIP 0031, *Why people matter*.

Any suggested improvement should be linked to a formally agreed objective, usually as a business benefit and, where possible, with the benefit quantified.

Process and procedure improvements

It is also important that during the 'Act' stage the service provider ensures the service management process and procedures still support the service provider's policies and that they deliver the outputs efficiently.

Service improvement policy

Improvements are so important to best practice service management that ISO/IEC 20000-1, 4.4 includes a requirement that *'there shall be a published policy on service improvement'*. The service improvement policy dictates the nature of the improvements to the service, by improvements to the processes that deliver the service, the people who follow the processes and the technology and systems used to automate the processes.

Some improvements are targeted on a specific service. For example, a service that is based on the use of an email system would benefit specifically from the improvements to:

- the capacity management process planning for the performance of the infrastructure used by the email service;

- incident management classification, changing so that any problem or incident affecting emails will always be high priority;
- continuity planning, incorporating faster retrieval of email files and the system, in the event of a major service outage.

Liaison and communications

It is advisable for those involved in day-to-day service management and service improvements to keep the customer and any suppliers aware of the policy on improvements. The policy provides a common direction on what the improvements should achieve.

Managers who are committed to improvements are also willing and able to take the time and effort to explain the policy. They can also explain how the processes and procedures that underpin the policies are affected. Each member of staff should understand how they are affected and what their individual contribution will be.

Non-compliance

The 'Act' stage corrects defects which may be non-compliances with the requirements of ISO/IEC 20000 or a failure to follow the agreed service management plan, i.e. 'Any non-compliance with the standard or the service management plans **shall** be remedied.'

Roles and responsibilities

As for all aspects of service management, there must be no ambiguity about who does what when for service improvements. This reduces localized improvements being acted upon without reference to the wider scope of service improvements, avoiding the risk of conflicting changes.

Example: Confusion on roles and responsibilities

A service provider had allocated responsibilities for processes and process improvements incrementally and on a rather haphazard basis. As a consequence, there was limited clarity on 'who did what'. This was further compounded by many localized improvements – in some cases done parochially but affecting the whole life cycle of a process and, via interfaces, affecting other processes.

Recognizing that this was unsatisfactory, a senior manager was tasked with becoming the 'senior responsible owner'.

This manager was able to cut across localized initiatives and pull together a coherent and much simpler matrix of process owners, delivery managers and service improvement specialists.

Once the service provider's management team and all the staff understood why this was being done and how they were affected, they generally accepted it. A few resisted the changes, but as the service improvements became a more logical and orderly set of changes, with each person being clear about who did what, even the diehards who had resisted it most strongly accepted that it was a better way of working.

Key point:

Doubt and confusion are a risk that, sooner or later, and generally sooner, causes deficiencies in processes, in the service and with the effective automation of processes. Knowing who does what is always an improvement.

Setting priorities

When, as is often the case, there are several suggested changes, each suggested change must be allocated a priority and must not be implemented without being formally agreed by a manager who has the correct level of authority. Service improvements are handled in the same way as any other change.

The priority must take into account the customer's interests – a change that does not directly or indirectly benefit the customer should be assessed to ensure that it is actually worthwhile making the improvement, as any improvement carries some risk that it will fail.

Any improvement must be assessed for implications on all processes, not simply the one that is to be improved.

Example: Assessing improvement priorities

A set of guidelines or rules on what improvements should be made first is an advantage for simplifying the setting of priorities for the PDCA cycle. Main criteria include:

- the customer's business needs;
- likely impact on customer satisfaction;
- policies that will be supported by the improvement;
- objectives that will be met;
- gains for service levels;
- costs and risks of the changes required for the improvements;
- costs and risks if the changes are not made;
- potential impact on other processes if one process is changed.

For example, if the incident management process is changed, this will have ramifications for problem management and service reporting. It could have implications for several other processes, including change management and service level management.

Control

When implementing improvements, it is necessary for the service provider to recognize that improvements must be controlled by the plan or plans produced during the 'Plan' stage of the PDCA cycle. This is included as a requirement in the 'Act' stage to ensure that improvements are not identified, agreed and implemented *ad hoc*, as this uncontrolled approach will undermine the PDCA cycle.

ISO/IEC 20000-1 also includes a requirement that there is a process covering the following stages for implementing improvements:

- identification;
- measurement;
- reporting on progress;
- management of the planned improvements.

The 'Act' stage must accommodate improvements being made locally, while still under the control of the PDCA cycle. These are improvements to a process where the improvement will have no direct or indirect impact on other processes.

Examples include:

- streamlining procedures within a team;
- improvements to incident data gathering from using scripts;
- altering the presentation of reports to make them easier to use;
- changing the process review frequency.

Other improvements that must be controlled are those that span processes, either by involving more than one process or a change to one process that has a direct or indirect impact on other processes. This may also affect more than one part of the service provider's organization and are normally coordinated and controlled in the PDCA cycle and not by an individual process owner. Risk assessment will help identify which category an improvement falls into.

Other requirements

The service provider is also required by ensure all types of improvement are considered and, if agreed, implemented. These include the following:

- collect and analyse data to baseline and benchmark the organization's capability to manage and deliver service management;
- identify, plan and implement improvements;
- consult with all parties involved;
- set targets for improvements in quality, costs and resource utilization;
- consider relevant inputs about improvements from all the service management processes;
- measure, report and communicate the service improvements;
- revise the service management policies, plans and procedures where necessary;
- ensure that all approved actions are delivered and that they achieve their intended objectives.

Baselining

A baseline is a snapshot of a service or of individual configuration items at a point in time. Baselining can cover the quality of service, service management processes, workloads managed, customer satisfaction with the service and cost-effectiveness of both the service and service management processes. Baselining can also include tracking changes in service quality over time, e.g. has the service really got worse, or has it really got more expensive? Also, if the service has changed, what else has changed? For example, service levels are linked to the workloads, support staff headcount and the extent of automation. It is advisable to baseline before and after major changes.

Being able to quantify the benefits is important as part of the 'lessons learned' and as a consequence, there is a requirement that the service is baselined before any significant change is made to the service. The improvements are then compared to the baseline, usually by repeating the baselining process. The planning of additional improvements will improve once practical experience has been gained on what can be achieved and how long it takes.

These requirements apply even if the change is made to a single process or where the change is being made to avoid the risk of a failure or to prevent a problem recurring. The baselining should not only look at any processes that are to be improved, but also others that may be indirectly affected, the service quality and service levels.

When baselining involves comparison with other organizations it is usually referred to as benchmarking.

Benchmarking

Benchmarking compares the services and service management processes of different organizations or different units within an organization. An audit against the requirements of ISO/IEC 20000 is benchmarking.

 ### Example: Major improvements

A pharmaceutical company decided to increase its focus in the problem management process as it was experiencing unprecedented support call volumes. Initially, the focus was on high priority high volume areas, but as more permanent fixes were implemented, other areas were able to receive attention. Within three months, the volume of support calls was reduced by 50%, freeing up valuable support staff for further problem management work and previously delayed service improvement projects.

Key point:

While there had to be an initial upfront investment of effort, the return on that investment was considerable.

Example metrics and audit evidence

The example metrics and audit evidence given in Tables 15 and 16 are illustrations only, for the reasons given in the section *Example metrics and audit evidence*, in Chapter 2.

Table 15 – Example metrics for the 'Act' stage of PDCA

Metric	Type of metric	Purpose and ISO/IEC 20000 objective
Service improvement policy	Currency and status of policy on service improvements	There shall be a published policy on service improvement
	Roles and responsibilities defined. Evidence of roles and responsibilities being acted upon as action plans, actions lists and actions completed	Roles and responsibilities for service improvement activities shall be clearly defined
Improvement progress reporting	Progress report. Actions identified and implemented as a result of the progress report	The organization shall have a process in place to identify, measure, report and manage improvement activities on an ongoing basis

Table 16 – Example audit evidence for requirements

Objective and requirement	Example audit evidence
Objective: To improve the effectiveness and efficiency of service delivery and management.	
All suggested service improvements **shall** be assessed, recorded, prioritized and authorized	Example input to the service improvement programme. Criteria for setting priorities. Authorization rules. Examples of authorized improvements being implemented
The organization **shall** perform activities to: e) consider relevant inputs about improvements from all the service management processes	Process and procedure for collection of suggestions improvements including: • Suggestions schemes • Service reviews • Meetings with customers • Analysis of service reports

CHAPTER 9

Planning and implementing new and changed services (ISO/IEC 20000-1, 5)

Introduction

ISO/IEC 20000 has specific requirements and recommendations for a service provider to ensure that new or changed services are deliverable and manageable at the right cost and service quality. Typical examples of such changes are introduction of a new service, closure of a service and major change to an existing service.

This chapter describes the key features and requirements of planning and implementing new or changed services to ensure that these services will be deliverable and manageable at the agreed cost and service quality.

The differences in scope between the process for planning and implementing new or changed services, and the change management process can be summarized as:

- planning new and changed services is a relatively major event, with implications for many processes and risks for other existing services;
- planning of new and changed services always involves a project (even if short-lived);
- planning for new or changed services should always be done in conjunction with the customer and normally at the instigation of the customer.

Context

Service providers may implement several new or changed services together with little understanding of the real impact on the overall service delivery and management. For example, the total cost of ownership (TCO) of a new service is three or four times more than estimated by the original project responsible for implementing the new service. In such cases, the service may go live with insufficient budget, resources, processes and automation. This has implications for service management as a whole as budget and resources may have to be diverted from other services.

The PDCA cycle shown in Figure 13 provides the context diagram for managing requests for new or changed services that may impact the service provider's overall capability to 'manage services'.

Planning a new or changed service

ISO/IEC 20000-1 requires that the service provider plans and agrees adequate funding and resources to make the changes for the new or changed service. Good scoping and clearly defined requirements are essential.

The level of planning for a new or changed service will be determined by:

- size and complexity of the change (e.g. is it a major change?);
- new 'one-off' service for a customer;
- new service to be transferred in from an external organization;
- whether staff will transfer in or out;
- whether it is a new service or a change to a service;
- how many people will use the service;
- whether the service is based on an internal or external solution or mix of these.

An auditor would expect to see that the level of planning is appropriate for the type of change. ISO/IEC 20000-1 requires the plans to include:

- staff recruitment/retraining;
- communication about the changes;
- formal closure of the services.

ISO/IEC 20000-2 provides recommendations for planning topics. This includes:

- the development and control of a specific service management plan;
- new scope for service management, including changes to the:
- service catalogue;
    - customers;
    - users;
    - locations;
    - business units;
    - suppliers;

- updates to the management system;
- updates to the service management framework including:
  - objectives;
  - policy;
  - processes,
  - procedures;
  - work instructions;
  - checklists;
  - templates
  - methods;
  - tools;
- organizational and role changes.

Impact assessment

The implementation of new or changed services must be planned and approved through formal change management, as described in BIP 0035, *Enabling change*. Assessment of the impact is vital. Examples are illustrated in Table 17.

Table 17 – Impact assessment for new or changed services

ISO/IEC 20000 requirement	Example of impact assessment questions
Impact on existing services	Will the service meet the business and customer expectations and requirements?
	Can the service levels be measured?
	Is the service aligned with the IT architecture?
	Are standard services and configurations used wherever possible?
	What are the risks to existing services?
	Is it possible to measure the expected results from the service?

Table 17 – Impact assessment for new or changed services (continued)

ISO/IEC 20000 requirement	Example of impact assessment questions
Impact on service management framework	Is there an impact on existing service management policies, processes, procedures, documents and records?
	Does the service comply with corporate governance, legal and regulatory requirements?
	Is it aligned with the service management scope, plans and requirements for delivering efficient and effective service?
	Can the service be managed and controlled across the supply chain?
Impact on cost	Is the estimated total cost of ownership acceptable?
	Has the budget been updated to reflect the change to the service management, operations and support budgets?
	Will there be an impact on the existing cost of running the service change, e.g. extra staff to do configuration management?
	Is a higher volume of incidents expected during first months of operation and how will this be funded?
	Are there any more opportunities for reducing costs?
Impact on the organization	Will the service deliver the estimated benefits?
	Is there any impact on capacity and staff resources, e.g. do we have the staff with the right skill sets and experience?
	Do we need to reorganize the teams to deliver the service?
	Does the change affect the scope of service management, e.g. by increasing the customer base or supported locations?
	Is there an impact on the service provider staff, e.g. staff may need to move locations, work different hours?
	Is there any impact on the customer organization?
	Are there implications for existing services, e.g. service level agreements, agreement on internal supporting services, contracts?
	Is there an impact on existing policies, processes or procedures?
	Is there any impact of not doing the change?
	Is there a good communication plan?

Table 17 – Impact assessment for new or changed services (continued)

ISO/IEC 20000 requirement	Example of impact assessment questions
Impact on technology	Does the new or changed service introduce new technology? If so, is there a plan for introducing the new technology?
	Is the new or changed service based on standard architectures, standard configurations and standard builds?
	Is the impact on capacity defined?
Commercial impact	Are the commercial and supplier management requirements and constraints addressed?
	Is there any additional impact on supplier management, contract management and their interfaces?
	Have suppliers been assessed for their capability to support and control the new or changed service?
	Have any contract changes been identified?

Example: Learning from a failed implementation

A logistics company is supported by an internal service provider. When a new financial service was implemented there were major issues and many related services were destabilized. There were complaints from the business, customers, users, business partners and suppliers. The company reviewed their process against the requirements of ISO/IEC 20000 and developed plans that included:

- defining the business and service management requirements;
- analysis of current capabilities;
- analysis of how the new service impacts the current services;
- risk analysis for additional changes;
- development of costed options for improvements;
- redesign of the unreliable service to deliver reliability;
- design of new or improved service reports;
- service acceptance criteria;
- communications plan on the proposed improvements.

New or improved documents placed under change, configuration and release management included:

- specifications for the new service and related services;
- service acceptance criteria;
- improvements to the IT strategy and architecture;
- revised service management framework;
- roles and responsibilities matrices;
- service catalogue, including closure of redundant services;
- supplier contracts and new internal service agreements;
- metrics, methods, tools and budget;
- service resource and staffing plan/training plan;
- communications plan.

The planned improvements were implemented after they had been tested and agreed, using best practice service management. This second attempt was on time and within budget.

The customer was pleased with the new business opportunity and the customer satisfaction was excellent. The IT staff were less stressed as they were very prepared for the change. Achieving ISO/IEC 20000 became a company goal.

Key point:

The service provider and their customer were able to quantify the benefits of adopting best practice service management specified by ISO/IEC 20000, not just in greater efficiency but in reduction in the overhead of managing a poor quality service and many complaints.

Links to the PDCA cycle

Where projects are responsible for introducing new services and making changes to existing services there will be an interface to the PDCA cycle. This includes projects that transition services or parts of services into or out of an organization, e.g. outsourcing, in-sourcing, off-shoring. The service provider should be involved in such projects and assign the necessary roles and resources to ensure that service changes do not unexpectedly degrade or impact the overall delivery of existing services.

An auditor will expect to see evidence of control of interfaces to key groups, e.g. programmes, projects, suppliers, development.

The service provider must assess the extent to which the service management requirements and practices will be met by any project.

There must be an agreed approach and plan to introduce a new or changed service, at the required time, in a known and documented configuration that meets the defined requirements. The service provider must be able to keep track of the configuration throughout the life cycle of the service. The plan provides input into the change management process to inform the impact and approval activities.

Transferring services from other organizations

Services may be transferred in several different ways:

*   out to a new supplier;
*   from one supplier to another;
*   back in from a supplier;
*   to or from an external organization.

The last category refers to an organization that has been providing services direct to the customer's organization and not direct to the service provider. This may be a transition by which the organization becomes a supplier to the service provider.

The service development life cycle

Planning for new or changed services will depend on the life cycle of the service and may vary depending on the customer or supplier. A typical life cycle for a service is initiation, requirements, acquisition, development, test, live and retirement. By understanding the life cycle of the service, it is easier to identify the intersections for change management and to plan when the configuration items should be placed under configuration management.

Good planning will ensure that the service provider's staff are actively involved in defining the service requirements and acceptance criteria early in the service development life cycle. This also ensures that the requirements and acceptance criteria are defined in line with the overall service management framework and plans. It is too late to define the acceptance criteria once the service has been developed.

Example metrics and audit evidence

The examples given in Tables 18 and 19 are only illustrations as each service provider may meet the requirements by using different metrics.

Table 18 – Example metrics for the new and changed services

Metric	Type of metric	Purpose and ISO/IEC 20000 objective
Change management records	Number and types of change that impact the capacity and performance overall	Effective information between the capacity management process and the change management process
	Analysis of changes impacting the capacity by service and by type of resource	Capacity and performance management for services as well as for all resources, reflecting a business view and business needs
Resource and performance reports, for agreed time intervals and as trends	Server space, compared to thresholds for maximum space usage	Tracking of capacity and performance for ongoing management and for input to the next version of the capacity management plan
	Response times for a test PC	
	Capacity of the telecommunications technology	
	Number of staff available to support business critical service and workload per person	

Table 19 – Example audit evidence for requirements

Objective and requirement	Example audit evidence
Objective: To ensure that new services and changes to services will be deliverable and manageable at the right cost and service quality.	
Proposals for new or changed services **shall** consider the cost, organizational, technical and commercial impact that could result from service delivery and management	Impact assessments by relevant parties
Planning and implementation **shall** include adequate funding and resources to make the changes needed for service delivery and management	Service change is reflected in budgets
The service provider **shall** report on the outcomes achieved by the new or changed service against those planned following its implementation	Service reports demonstrate: • the impact of the service change on incident and problem management • achievements against planned service levels

Appendix A

ISO/IEC 20000 requirements in summary

It is important to refer to ISO/IEC 20000-1 and ISO/IEC 20000-2 and not rely on the abstract given here, which only covers those parts of ISO/IEC 20000 that are particularly pertinent to the topics in the scope of this book.

All publications in the 'Achieving ISO/IEC 20000' series feature similar tables that cover other requirements in the same way. Each requirement (signified by the use of the verb '**shall**') is supplemented by informative commentary based on the details in ISO/IEC 20000-2 and related publications.

The requirements and recommendations that are most relevant to integrated service management are not found in a single clause, or even in two or three clauses. Integrated service management is, perhaps more than any other aspect of service management, the end result of many best practices, and of meeting many requirements and adopting many recommendations. Integrated service management does, however, represent some of the major benefits of service management, and conversely, represents some of the greatest challenges for a service provider to achieve when aiming for ISO/IEC 20000.

Table A.1 – ISO/IEC 20000 requirements and recommendations with informative commentary/guidance

ISO/IEC 20000-1 requirements	ISO/IEC 20000-2 recommendations (*italics*) and additional commentary (**bold**)
3. Requirements for a management system	
Objective: To provide a management system, including policies and a framework to enable the effective management and implementation of all IT services.	
Clause 3.1: Management responsibility	
Through leadership and actions, top/executive management shall provide evidence of its commitment to developing, implementing and improving its service management capability within the context of the organization's business and customers' requirements.	*The role of management in ensuring best practice processes are adopted and sustained is fundamental for any service provider to meet the requirements of ISO/IEC 20000-1.*
Management **shall:** a) establish the service management policy, objectives and plans; b) communicate the importance of meeting the service management objectives and the need for continual improvement; c) ensure that customer requirements are determined and are met with the aim of improving customer satisfaction; d) appoint a member of management responsible for the co-ordination and management of all services;	*To ensure commitment, an owner at senior level **should** be identified as being responsible for service management plans.* *This senior responsible owner **should** be accountable for the overall delivery of the service management plan.*

ISO/IEC 20000-1 requirements	ISO/IEC 20000-2 recommendations (*italics*) and additional commentary (**bold**)
e) determine and provide resources to plan, implement, monitor, review and improve service delivery and management, e.g. recruit appropriate staff, manage staff turnover; f) manage risks to the service management organization and services; and g) conduct reviews of service management, at planned intervals, to ensure continuing suitability, adequacy and effectiveness.	*The senior responsible owner's role* **should** *encompass resourcing for any continual or project-based service improvement activities.* *The senior responsible owner* **should** *be supported by a decision-taking group with sufficient authority to define policy and to enforce its decisions.*

Clause 3.2: Documentation requirements. This is included in BIP 0030, *Management decisions and documentation.*

Clause 3.3: Competence, awareness and training. This is included in BIP 0032, *Why people matter.*

Table A.2 – ISO/IEC 20000 requirements and recommendations with informative commentary/guidance

ISO/IEC 20000-1 requirements	ISO/IEC 20000-2 recommendations (*italics*) and additional commentary (**bold**)
4. Planning and implementing service management **An overview of PDCA cycle has not been included in this table as it is neither recommendations nor requirements.** **4.1 Plan service management (Plan)** *Objective: To plan the implementation and delivery of service management.* The NOTE and figure on the PDCA cycle is included Chapter 4 and is not duplicated here.	
Service management **shall** be planned. The plans **shall** at a minimum define: a) the scope of the service provider's service management; b) the objectives and requirements that are to be achieved by service management; c) the processes that are to be executed; d) the framework of management roles and responsibilities, including the senior responsible owner, process owner and management of suppliers; e) the interfaces between service management processes and the manner in which the activities are to be co-ordinated; f) the approach to be taken in identifying, assessing and managing issues and risks to the achievement of the defined objectives;	*Scope of service management* *The scope of service management* **should** *be defined as part of the service management plan. For example, it may be defined by:* *a) organization;* *b) location;* *c) service.* *Management* **should** *define the scope as part of their management responsibilities (and as part of the service management plan).*

ISO/IEC 20000-1 requirements	ISO/IEC 20000-2 recommendations (*italics*) and additional commentary (**bold**)
g) the approach for interfacing to projects that are creating or modifying services; h) the resources, facilities and budget necessary to achieve the defined objectives; i) tools as appropriate to support the processes; and j) how the quality of the service will be managed, audited and improved.	*The scope **should** then be checked for suitability under ISO/IEC 20000-1.* NOTE *Planning for operational changes is described in 9.3. (This refers to ISO/IEC 20000-2, 9.3.)*
There **shall** be clear management direction and documented responsibilities for reviewing, authorising, communicating, implementing and maintaining the plans.	*Multiple service management plans may be used in place of one large plan or programme. Where this is the case the underlying service management processes **should** be consistent with each other.* *It **should** also be possible to demonstrate how each planning requirement is managed by linking it to the corresponding roles, responsibilities and procedures.* *Service management planning **should** form part of the process for translating customers' requirements and senior management intentions into services, and for providing a route map for directing progress.*
Any process specific plans produced **shall** be compatible with this service management plan.	*A service management plan **should** encompass:* *a) implementation of service management (or part of service management);* *b) delivery of service management processes;* *c) changes to service management processes;* *d) improvements to service management processes;* *e) new services (to the extent that they affect processes within the agreed scope of service management).*

ISO/IEC 20000-2 recommendations (*italics*) and additional commentary (bold)

Events to be considered

The service management plan should *cater for service management process and service changes triggered by events such as:*

a) service improvement;

b) service changes;

c) infrastructure standardization;

d) changes to legislation;

e) regulatory changes, e.g. local tax rate changes;

f) deregulation or regulation of industries;

g) mergers and acquisitions.

Scope and contents of the plan

A service management plan **should** *define:*

a) the scope of the service provider's service management;

b) the objectives and requirements that are to be achieved by service management;

c) the resource, facilities and budgets necessary to achieve the defined objectives;

d) the framework of management roles and responsibilities, including the senior responsible owner, process owners and management of suppliers;

e) the interfaces between service management processes and the manner in which activities and/or processes are to be coordinated;

f) the approach to be taken in identifying, assessing and managing issues risks so the achievement of the defined objectives;

ISO/IEC 20000-1 requirements

112

ISO/IEC 20000-1 requirements

ISO/IEC 20000-2 recommendations (*italics*) and additional commentary (**bold**)

g) a resource schedule expressed in terms of the dates on which funds, skills, and resources <u>*should*</u> *be available;*

h) the approach to changing the plan and the service defined by the plan;

i) how the service provider will demonstrate continuing quality control (e.g. interim audits);

j) the processes that are to be executed;

k) tools as appropriate to support the processes.

Table A.3 – ISO/IEC 20000 requirements and recommendations with informative commentary/guidance

ISO/IEC 20000-1 requirements	ISO/IEC 20000-2 recommendations (*italics*) and additional commentary (**bold**)
4. Planning and implementing service management **4.2 Implement service management and provide the services (Do)** *Objective: To implement the service management objectives and plan.*	
The service provider **shall** implement the service management plan to manage and deliver the services, including: a) allocation of funds and budgets; b) allocation of roles and responsibilities; c) documenting and maintaining the policies, plans, procedures and definitions for each process or set of processes; d) identification and management of risks to the service; e) managing teams, e.g. recruiting and developing appropriate staff and managing staff continuity; f) managing facilities and budget; g) managing the teams including service desk and operations; h) reporting progress against the plans; and i) co-ordination of service management processes.	*Attainment of best practice service management processes capable of meeting the requirements of ISO/IEC 20000 will not be achieved if the original services do not meet the requirements outlined for implementation in ISO/IEC 20000 Part 1.* *Once implemented the service and service management processes **should** be maintained.* *NOTE The person that is appropriate for the planning and initial implementation may not be suitable for the ongoing operation.*

Table A.4 – ISO/IEC 20000 requirements and recommendations with informative commentary/guidance

ISO/IEC 20000-1 requirements	ISO/IEC 20000-2 recommendations (*italics*) and additional commentary (**bold**)
4. Planning and implementing service management	
NOTE See also Introduction.	
4.3 Monitoring, measuring and reviewing (Check)	
Objective: To monitor, measure and review that the service management objectives and plan are being achieved.	
The service provider **shall** apply suitable methods for monitoring and, where applicable, measurement of the service management processes.	*The service provider **should** plan and implement the monitoring, measurement and analysis and review of the service, the service management processes and associated systems.*
These methods **shall** demonstrate the ability of the processes to achieve planned results.	*Items that **should** be monitored, measured and reviewed include:* *a) achievement against defined service targets;* *b) customer satisfaction;* *c) resource utilization;* *d) trends;* *e) major non-conformities;* *f) achievement against defined service targets*
Management **shall** conduct reviews at planned intervals to determine whether the service management requirements: a) conform with the service management plan and to the requirements of this standard; and b) are effectively implemented and maintained.	*The results of the analysis **should** provide input to a plan for improving the service.*

115

ISO/IEC 20000-2 recommendations (*italics*) and additional commentary (**bold**)

As well as service management activities on measurement and analysis, senior management may need to make use of internal audits and other checks.

When deciding the frequency of such internal audits and checks, the degree of risk involved in a process, its frequency of operation and its past history of problems are among the factors that **should** *be taken into account.*

Internal audits and checks **should** *be planned, carried out and competently recorded.*

ISO/IEC 20000-1 requirements

An audit programme **shall** be planned, taking into consideration the status and importance of the processes and areas to be audited, as well as the results of previous audits.

The audit criteria, scope, frequency and methods **shall** be defined in a procedure.

The selection of auditors and conduct of audits **shall** ensure objectivity and impartiality of the audit process.

Auditors **shall** not audit their own work.

The objective of service management reviews, assessments and audits **shall** be recorded together with the findings of such audits and reviews and any remedial actions identified.

Any significant areas of non-compliance or concern **shall** be communicated to relevant parties.

Table A.5 – ISO/IEC 20000 requirements and recommendations with informative commentary/guidance

ISO/IEC 20000-1 requirements	ISO/IEC 20000-2 recommendations (*italics*) and additional commentary (**bold**)
4. Planning and implementing service management NOTE See also Introduction. **4.4 Continual improvement (Act)** *Objective: To improve the effectiveness and efficiency of service delivery and management.* **Policy** There **shall** be a published policy on service improvement. Any non-compliance with the standard or the service management plans **shall** be remedied. Roles and responsibilities for service improvement activities **shall** be clearly defined.	**Policy** *Service providers* **should** *recognize that there is always the potential to make delivery of services more effective and efficient.* *There* **should** *be a published policy on service quality and improvement.* *All those involved in service management and service improvement* **should** *be aware of the service quality policy and their personal contribution to the achievement of the objectives laid out within this policy.* *In particular all the service provider's staff involved in service management* **should** *have a detailed understanding of the implications of this on service management processes.* *There* **should** *be effective liaison within the service provider's own management structure, the customers and the service provider's suppliers on matters affecting service quality and customer requirements.*

117

ISO/IEC 20000-2 recommendations (*italics*) and additional commentary (**bold**)

Planning for service improvements

*Service providers **should** adopt a methodical and coordinated approach to service improvement to meet the requirements of the policy, from their own and from their customer's perspective.*

*Before implementing a plan for improving the service, service quality and levels **should** be recorded as a baseline against which the actual improvements can be compared.*

*The actual improvement **should** be compared to the predicted improvement to assess the effectiveness of the change.*

ISO/IEC 20000-1 requirements

Management of improvements

All suggested service improvements **shall** be assessed, recorded, prioritized and authorized.

A plan **shall** be used to control the activity.

The service provider **shall** have a process in place to identify, measure, report and manage improvement activities on an ongoing basis.

This **shall** include:

a) improvements to an individual process that can be implemented by the process owner with the usual staff resources, e.g. performing individual corrective and preventive actions; and

b) improvements across the organization or across more than one process.

Activities

The service provider **shall** perform activities to:

a) collect and analyse data to baseline and benchmark the service provider's capability to manage and deliver service and service management processes;

ISO/IEC 20000-1 requirements

b) identify, plan and implement improvements;

c) consult with all parties involved;

d) set targets for improvements in quality, costs and resource utilization;

e) consider relevant inputs about improvements from all the service management processes;

f) measure, report and communicate the service improvements;

g) revise the service management policies, processes, procedures and plans where necessary; and

h) ensure that all approved actions are delivered and that they achieve their intended objectives.

ISO/IEC 20000-2 recommendations (*italics*) and additional commentary (**bold**)

NOTE 1 Service improvement requirements can come from all processes.

Service providers should encourage their staff and customers to suggest ways of improving services.

NOTE 2 This may be done using suggestion schemes, quality circles, user groups and liaison meetings.

Service improvement targets should be measurable, linked to business objectives and documented in the plan.

Service improvement should be actively managed and progress should be monitored against formally agreed objectives.

Table A.6 – ISO/IEC 20000 requirements and recommendations with informative commentary/guidance

ISO/IEC 20000-1 requirements	ISO/IEC 20000-2 recommendations (*italics*) and additional commentary (**bold**)
5. Planning and implementing new or changed services	
Objective: To ensure that new services and changes to services will be deliverable and manageable at the agreed cost and service quality.	
	Planning and implementing new or changed services
	Topics for consideration
	Planning for new or changed services **should** *include reviewing:*
	a) budgets;
	b) staff resources;
	c) existing service levels;
	d) SLAs and other targets or service commitments;
	e) existing service management processes, procedures and documentation;
	f) the scope of service management, including the implementation of service management processes previously excluded from the scope.
Proposals for new or changed services **shall** consider the cost, organizational, technical and commercial impact that could result from service delivery and management.	
	Change records
	All service changes **should** *be reflected in Change Management records. This includes plans for:*
	a) staff recruitment/retraining;
	b) relocation;
The implementation of new or changed services, including closure of a service, **shall** be planned and approved through formal change management.	

ISO/IEC 20000-1 requirements	ISO/IEC 20000-2 recommendations (*italics*) and additional commentary (**bold**)
	c) user training; d) communications about the changes; e) changes to the nature of the technology supported; f) formal closure of services.
The planning and implementation **shall** include adequate funding and resources to make the changes needed for service delivery and management.	
The plans **shall** include: a) the roles and responsibilities for implementing, operating and maintaining the new or changed service including activities to be performed by customers and suppliers; b) changes to the existing service management framework and services; c) communication to the relevant parties; d) new or changed contracts and agreements to align with the changes in business need; e) manpower and recruitment requirements; f) skills and training requirements, e.g. users, technical support;	

ISO/IEC 20000-2 recommendations (*italics*) and additional commentary (bold)

ISO/IEC 20000-1 requirements

g) processes, measures, methods and tools to be used in connection with the new or changed service, e.g. capacity management, financial management;

h) budgets and time-scales;

i) service acceptance criteria; and

j) the expected outcomes from operating the new service expressed in measurable terms.

New or changed services **shall** be accepted by the service provider before being implemented into the live environment.

The service provider **shall** report on the outcomes achieved by the new or changed service against those planned following its implementation.

A post implementation review comparing actual outcomes against those planned, **shall** be performed through the change management process.

Bibliography and further information

Standards

BS 0-3, *A standard for standards — Part 3: Specification for structure, drafting and presentation*

ISO/IEC Directives Part 2, *Rules for the structure and drafting of International Standards*

ISO 9000, *Quality management systems — Fundamentals and vocabulary*

ISO 9001, *Quality management systems — Requirements*

ISO/IEC 17799, *Information technology — Security techniques — Code of practice for information security management*

ISO/IEC 20000-1, *Information technology — Service management — Part 1: Specification*

ISO/IEC 20000-2, *Information technology — Service management — Part 2: Code of practice*

ISO/IEC 27001, *Information technology — Security techniques — Information security management systems — Requirements*

BSI books

BIP 0005, *A manager's guide to service management*

BIP 0015, *IT service management — Self-assessment workbook*

BIP 0008, *Code of practice for legal admissibility and evidential weight of information stored electronically*

PAS 56, *Guide to business continuity management*

Security information

BIP 0070, *Information security compilation on CD-ROM*

BIP 0071, *Guidelines on requirements and preparation for certification based on ISO/IEC 27001*

BIP 0072, *Are you ready for an ISMS audit based on ISO/IEC 27001?*

BIP 0073, *Guide to the implementation and auditing of ISMS controls based on ISO/IEC 27001*

BIP 0074, *Measuring the effectiveness of your ISMS implementations based on ISO/IEC 27001*

Other resources

British Computer Society: www.bcs.org.uk

British Computer Society Configuration Management Specialist Group: www.bcs-cmsg.org.uk

The IT Service Management Forum (itSMF): www.itsmf.com

EXIN: www.exin.nl

Information Systems Examinations Board (ISEB): www.bcs.org.uk/iseb

The Office of Government Commerce: www.ogc.gov.uk

IT Infrastructure Library (ITIL): www.itil.co.uk

BOOKS IN THE
'ACHIEVING ISO/IEC 20000' SERIES

There are ten books in the 'Achieving ISO/IEC 20000' series. Each book in the series includes an abstract of ISO/IEC 20000 that is most relevant to the topic of the book, as well as useful contacts and sources of supporting information. These books can be purchased through the BSI website at www.bsi-global.com.

BIP 0030, *Management decisions and documentation*

This book covers: the background to ISO/IEC 20000; a comparison to other standards and best practice material; compliance and certification audits; the scope of service management; building the business case for achieving ISO/IEC 20000; preparation for an audit; and using ISO/IEC 20000 to select your supplier. Important terms that are used in management system standards, where the exact meaning of terms is important to the correct interpretation of the standard, are also explained, including the differences between the terms '<u>shall</u>', '<u>should</u>' and notes. This book also covers the requirements and recommendations for documents and records, which is a management responsibility requirement in clause 3.2 of ISO/IEC 20000-1.

BIP 0031, *Why people matter*

This book covers the roles and responsibilities of management and process owners, and explains the importance of management commitment to best practice service management, mapping onto the requirements and recommendations of clause 3.1 of ISO/IEC 20000, *Management responsibility*. The book also covers the importance of motivation, training and career development as well as tips and techniques, mapping onto the requirements of clause 3.3 of ISO/IEC 20000-1, *Competence, awareness and training*.

BIP 0032, *Making metrics work*

This book gives a practical view of why metrics and service reports are so important to the delivery of an effective service and to service improvements. It describes the types, the design, target audiences and documentation of metrics used in the service reporting process, covered by the requirements of clauses 4 and 6.2 of ISO/IEC 20000-1, *Plan-Do-Check-Act (PDCA) cycle* and *Service reporting*. Useful tips, techniques and example metrics are included.

BIP 0033, *Managing end-to-end service*

This book describes the supply chains that are commonly managed by service level management, business relationship management and supplier management, which are the requirements in clauses 6.1 and 7 of ISO/IEC 20000-1. It describes the interfaces between suppliers, the service provider and one or many customers. This book also includes useful tips for aspects of end-to-end service, such as the role of service level agreements (SLAs), service reviews, customer satisfaction and complaints procedures.

BIP 0034, *Finance for service managers*

This book covers *Budgeting and accounting for IT services* based on clause 6.4 of ISO/IEC 20000. It introduces financial terms that may be unfamiliar to service management specialists, which will help with understanding the requirements and recommendations. It also covers the relationship between budgeting, accounting and charging, and outlines the importance of service management processes in regulatory compliance.

BIP 0035, *Enabling change*

This book covers the configuration, change management and release management processes which are contained in clauses 9 and 10 of ISO/IEC 20000. It compares the three processes and describes how they interface with each other, and gives advice on the requirements and recommendations of ISO/IEC 20000, example metrics and audit evidence. This book also includes practical advice on meeting the ISO/IEC 20000 requirements on the roles and responsibilities of those involved.

BIP 0036, *Keeping the service going*

This book covers the service continuity and availability management, incident management and problem management processes, which are contained in clauses 6.3 and 8 of ISO/IEC 20000. It explains the role of these processes in keeping the customer's service going, ranging from continuity planning through to the fast-fixing of incidents. It compares the processes and describes how they interface with each other. It includes example metrics and audit evidence, with practical tips and techniques that will help a service provider achieve the requirements.

BIP 0037, *Capacity management*

This book covers the requirements for the capacity management process in clause 6.5 of ISO/IEC 20000. It describes the capacity management process and its role as a link between business plans, workloads, capacity and performance). It also covers the planning required to ensure a service provider is able to deliver a service that allows the customer's business to operate effectively. The book describes capacity management for all types of resources within the scope of service management.

BIP 0038, *Integrated service management*

The opening paragraph of ISO/IEC 20000-1 states that '*This standard promotes the adoption of an integrated process approach to effectively deliver managed services to meet the business and customer requirements*'. This book reflects the importance placed by ISO/IEC 20000 on understanding the interfaces between processes, and how the interfaces are managed so that service management processes are fully integrated. It also reflects the top-down management system approach that is fundamental to ISO/IEC 20000. This book describes how understanding and meeting the requirements of ISO/IEC 20000 gives better control, greater efficiency and opportunities for improvements.

BIP 0039, *The differences between BS 15000 and ISO/IEC 20000*

This book will be of particular interest to those who have used BS 15000 for service improvements, audits or training and need to update their material to reflect the ISO/IEC 20000 standard. ISO/IEC 20000 was based on BS 15000, and this book provides a detailed comparison of ISO/IEC 20000 and BS 15000, for both Parts 1 and 2. It shows the differences in structure, clause numbering and references. The core of this book is a series of tables detailing the changes to the requirements and recommendations clause-by-clause, as well as any re-wording that has been provided to give clarification for an international audience. It includes an explanation of why the changes were made and the implications of each of the changes. This book is based on the material produced by the Project Editor during the drafting of both Parts 1 and 2 of ISO/IEC 20000.